Beatrix Potter

Her Life in the
Lake District

Beatrix Potter

Her Life in the Lake District

by

W R Mitchell

Hill Top, Near Sawrey

CASTLEBERG
1998

For
WILLOW TAYLOR
who remembers the real
Beatrix Potter

Enlarged and Revised Edition of
"Beatrix Potter Remembered"

A **Castleberg** Book.

First published in the United Kingdom in 1998.

Copyright © W R Mitchell 1998.

The moral right of the author has been asserted.

ISBN 1 871064 82 1

Typeset in ITC Clearface, printed and bound in the United Kingdom by
Lamberts Print & Design, Station Road, Settle, North Yorkshire, BD24 9AA.

Published by Castleberg, 18 Yealand Avenue, Giggleswick, Settle,
North Yorkshire, BD24 0AY.

Contents

ILLUSTRATIONS

Cover painting by Janet Rawlins

Drawings by Edward Jeffrey, mostly based on photographs by the author.

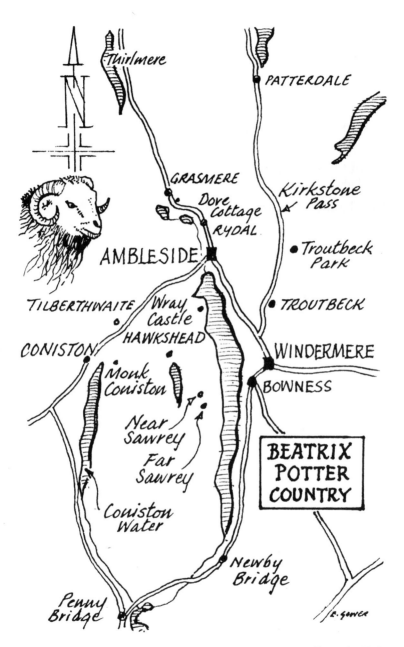

Thirlmere

PATTERDALE

GRASMERE

Dove
Cottage

RYDAL

Kirkstone
Pass

AMBLESIDE

Troutbeck
Park

TILBERTHWAITE

Wray
Castle

TROUTBECK

HAWKSHEAD

CONISTON

WINDERMERE

Monk
Coniston

BOWNESS

Near
Sawrey

Far
Sawrey

BEATRIX
POTTER
COUNTRY

Coniston
Water

Newby
Bridge

Penny
Bridge

E. Gower

Drawn by E. Gower

6

Foreword

to the 1987 edition

by Mary E Burkett

formerly Director of Abbot Hall, Kendal

BEATRIX POTTER's name bears with it an air of mystery because it is associated with a scientist, a sheep-farmer, an intellectual as well as that of an inspired illustrator and author of children's tales. Many books have been written about her stating emphatically what sort of a person she was. But since then a secret diary has come to light which reveals her as an even more enigmatic figure.

She achieved a style of animal painting which is remarkable not only in its simplicity and purity but in its lack of sentimentality. The animals are, in spite of their clothes, tough little creatures and her awareness of form and action is clearly shown in their obvious character. The lack of pretension and false pomp is clearly illustrated by her indifference to the clothes she wore.

Her popularity, however, increases all the time. When we staged our first exhibition of her work at Abbot Hall, Kendal, in February and March 1966, we had more people visiting the gallery than we had in mid-summer despite the weather. They wanted to know what sort of a person she really was.

There are still some people in the Lake District who remember her, and even a few who worked for her. This anthology of people's memories of her will add to the ever-increasing store of information about her. It is an excellent idea of Bill Mitchell, the author, to have accumulated these recollections of 30 or more years of her life and I wish it every success.

Foreword

to the 1998 edition
by Judy Taylor

IT IS ELEVEN years since the first edition of this very personal book was published. Then called *Beatrix Potter Remembered*, it has been unavailable for far too long. During those intervening years, interest in the life of the extraordinary woman who is the book's subject has spread across the world and, indeed, continues to grow as every year new discoveries - of letters, diaries, pictures - offer Beatrix Potter biographers and admirers previously unknown details of her life.

Sadly, the small band of people who met and knew Beatrix Potter is fast dwindling, which makes Bill Mitchell's interviews, which he began in 1955 and has often transcribed in the dialect of the area, into snippets of history. They provide us with a realistic and down-to-earth picture of what the people of the Lake District thought of this woman from London, who not only chose to make her home amongst them for thirty years but also competed with them in their traditional farming life. The fact that everyone does not agree adds considerably to the interest and entertainment.

Acknowledgements

THANKS are extended to past or present residents of the Lake District for assistance during the compilation of this book. Special help was given by Josephina Banner, Anthony Benson, Mrs Frank Birkett, Winifrid Bonney Bower, Charlie Brown, Mary Burkett, John Fishwick, Nigel Holmes, Ted Jackson, National Trust, Radio Cumbria, Janet Rawlins, Annie Richards, Tom Storey, Willow Taylor, Amanda Thistlethwaite, Lydia Thomas, Mrs Gordon Tyson, William Waddington, Jean Warren, Dr J N Warren, C T Williamson.

Beatrix Potter

Your eyes were always summer.
Common sense, surprise and fun
burnished your internal sun,
lighting your books. Here we find
a cradling-comfort, cats purr
warmth, recognising objects
homely, simple as bee skeps,
tea-pots, feathers, water-butts,
nests with eggs, a fox who struts
sneering, across our dreaming,
first lesson about deceiving.

Clogs on feet, dressed in tweed
conversing with farmers, owt
about sheep, but Herdwicks' breed,
you judged. There can be nowt
worth knowing, you didn't know,
which is why my children's
children stand at my bookshelf
and find their hands go
to Beatrix Potter.

Lydia Thomas

Candid Comments

Among the little books which have become as much a manifestation of autumn as falling leaves, one looks first for whatever Miss Beatrix Potter gives.
The Times Literary Supplement, September, 1904.

There is something very lovable about the silly sheep and the simple old-fashioned talk of those who work the soil and the flock.
Beatrix Potter, writing to a friend, quoted by John Heelis, 1993.

It's gay weather for the likes of thee and me, missus.
A tramp, speaking to Beatrix Potter, whom he met plodding home in the rain.

Cousin Beatie's stern exterior and firm, almost forbidding manner hid many fears which she had carried within her since her childhood.
Ulla Hyde Parker, her cousin's wife.

Beatrix Potter was eccentric, but if one respected her idiosyncrasies and her desire for privacy she was friendly and kind.
Mrs M R Ormerod, of Reading, in the Radio Times, May 13, 1971.

She was rather reserved. Quiet. But spoke her mind when she did speak.
Tom Storey, her shepherd at Hill Top.

She was so great in her tiny way. She was a little bundle of charm and cleverness and great wisdom.
Josephina Banner.

Her life seems to have held an element of magic and whose happiest years were spent in this glorious countryside that seems to blend perfectly the magical and the real.
Radio Cumbria.

My brother and I were born in London. . .but our descent - our interests and our joy - was in the the north country.
Beatrix Potter.

An Introduction

IN THE SUMMER of 1896, Rupert Potter of Bolton Gardens, London, rented a mini-mansion in the village of Far Sawrey, near Hawkshead, intent on spending several of the summer weeks with his family in the English Lake District. Rupert, a barrister who was wealthy enough never to have practised, and his wife Helen, were talented but serious minded. Their two children, Beatrix and Bertram, had a repressed Victorian childhood. To Beatrix, a girl with a lively, inquisitive mind, not being able to leave the house when she wished, nor to mix with other children, turned her attention to resources near at hand and to the companionship of several household pets.

Their Lakeland retreat in that summer of 1896 was Lakefield, overlooking floriferous meadows extending to the reedy edges of Esthwaite Water. The Sawrey district, with its gentle landscape, between

Windermere and Coniston Water, offered a freedom Beatrix had not hitherto imagined, even during family holidays in Scotland and northern Lakeland. She was old enough to be able to drive herself about the district in a pony and trap. She had the companionship of Don, a dog of the wiry collie breed. When the weeks of holidaymaking ended, and she was back in the constrictions of London, she confided to her journal, using a code which was not to be "broken" until well after her death: "It is as nearly perfect a little place as I ever lived in."

Beatrix eventually asserted her independence by buying one of the small farms of Sawrey. This was Hill Top, tucked out of sight of the world behind the Tower Bank Arms, but backing on to fields and woods. Her parents were not made aware of her desire for independence. She persuaded them that Hill Top was an investment. Yet the unpretentious farmhouse, with its flagged ground floor, its funny old fireplace and the water-butts to intercept the heavy Lakeland rainfall, became the focal point for her aspirations.

When, in 1913, Beatrix was married to Willie Heelis, she retained Hill Top exactly as it was and the happy couple set up home in Castle Cottage, which was tucked away in a quiet spot just off Stony Lane. For the thirty years of her marriage, Beatrix was blissfully in tune with Willie Heelis, the gentle Lakeland solicitor, and with the Lakeland landscape, its people and animal life. This second half of Beatrix's life is the period covered by my book. It is based on "taped" conversations with people who knew Beatrix and Willie. They have provided sidelights on the woman who has become one of the best-known authors and whose little books for little children about the adventures of little animals continue to enchant.

In the second phase of her life, Beatrix had a serious intent - to preserve. She bought up land and property, intending some day that it would be maintained in an unspoilt state by the National Trust, one of the founders of which had been Hardwicke Drummond Rawnsley, a

Lakeland clergyman who had become a close friend of the Potter family. During her marriage, the considerable artistic powers which had produced a run of classic children's books were on the wane. She who had fascinated children and also their parents with tales about Peter Rabbit, Tom Kitten, Jeremy Fisher, Jemima Puddleduck, and many another engaging characters, now used her wit and energy in farming. It was, as she herself observed, a shift from paper-book animals to real animals. She slowed down the heady rush of progress in this sylvan part of North Lancashire by preserving old buildings, old ways.

The Potters were "not short of bob or two", to quote a northern saying. Her grandfather's fortunes were founded on calico printing in Lancashire. His second son, Beatrix's father, became a London barrister who married into "brass", his bride being Helen Leech, daughter of a cotton merchant from Stalybridge. Beatrix, a Londoner, never quite became "yan of us" in her chosen community of Near Sawrey, and at times she annoyed local people, especially the farmers, through her frequent purchases of land which normally would have been bought up by her neighbours. Beatrix was indifferent to their grumbling and continued to make practical use of information given to her, on the quiet, by her husband. Willie had his fingers firmly on the pulse of local business life. At times, she could be so self-seeking her manner bordered on callousness. A field she purchased half way up Ferry Hill became hers with the proviso that she would provide a seat on which people might rest and admire a view of Windermere in its setting of wooded hills and bare fells. Beatrix did not provide that seat. The idea smacked too much of tourism.

To an ordinary villager, "scratting" for a living in a district where poverty knocked on most of the doors, Beatrix was a local farmer who wrote books. You might buy them in the village shop. Or, if you caught her eye, or took her fancy, she might even give you one, neatly autographed. Beatrix, an attractive lass, became a small, dumpy, round-

13

shouldered, tweed-clad figure, an oddity as she bustled about the farm-yard with a hessian apron round her waist and clogs on her feet. She would set off for the shop with a bonnet on her head and a tattered shawl round her shoulders. Always, there were shiny clogs peeping out from beneath her voluminous skirt. Sawrey, and other Lakeland villages, re-sounded to the clatter of clog-irons. Many children went to school in clogs. Farmers wore clogs to "turn t'snow broth" and women had warm feet when wearing clogs in their draughty, slate-flagged kitchens.

Beatrix was the classic case of "still waters run deep". She kept herself to herself. The books she had written comprised the public side of Beatrix Potter but who, among her contemporaries, could have guessed at an intensely private life which one day would be revealed when Leslie Linder "cracked" the code of the journal she kept during her formative years - a record of her inner thoughts which would run to over two hundred thousand words? The funny old lady had been a pretty little girl who craved affection but did not receive it in a straight-laced upper middle class home where children were "to be seen and not heard".

Thrown back largely on her own resources, Beatrix developed a range of interests, including natural history and art. She dissected animals to study their anatomy, knowledge for its own sake which eventually was to give realism to her water-colour sketches of animals. She grew up in a Victorian period when there was a morbid interest in death and when naturalists were dissecting, describing and classifying the animal world. Beatrix hoped to take up scientific work but was discouraged when mycological research papers she submitted to the Linnean Society were forcibly rejected. During one Scottish holiday, Beatrix met Charlie McIntosh, an amateur naturalist. He inspired in her a deeper fascination with the natural world. By 1896, she was an accomplished naturalist.

Who among those who knew only her little books could have imagined with what charm and interest she corresponded chattily with her friends, the topics of those letters being mainly about farmstock or the

14

state of the weather? Now and again there were indications of stress, such as the unreasonable demands made on her by Helen, an aged, unfeeling mother, who lingered on well into the nineties. Beatrix, having settled her in a large house on the Westmorland side of the lake, made great efforts to visit her, trudging from Sawrey to the ferry and hoping to find that on the other side her mother's carriage was waiting. Mother seemed to take a perverse pleasure in not sending it. On arriving at mother's home, she was often shown up in front of the servants. In earlier times, a clip-clop of horse's hooves at Sawrey on a Wednesday afternoon had signified the approach of the carriage bearing Beatrix's unsmiling mother for tea. Beatrix never drove a car but had the means to purchase one and to employ a chauffeur. Willie Heelis, her husband, was an unenthusiastic driver, who tended to grate the gears.

Beatrix's way of life, so different from the Lakeland norm, kept the tongues of local gossips busy. It was widely believed that in her spinsterhood, she sometimes went to bed with a sheep in lieu of a warming-pan or stone bottle. This was, of course, untrue, though believable, for the newly-wed Beatrix did take a sick piglet into the conjugal bed for the night. (The piglet made a good recovery). Mary Rogerson, the housekeeper at Castle Cottage, where Beatrix and Willie lived, recalled when Beatrix's pet sow, Sally, followed her around, sometimes even entering the dining room. Mercifully, it was house-trained.

When in an especially lively mood, Beatrix persuaded her Pekingese dogs, Tzusee and Chuleh, to balance sugar lumps on their noses. They were capable of dancing in circles. Beatrix also had a Pomeranian which she called Pom Ally. Josephina Banner, who knew Beatrix well, told me: "She enjoyed life, rather like a schoolboy might enjoy a day out. She had that splendid receptivity to life...She was so cute - and she knew she was cute. She knew she looked just like one of her little animals." She was also community-minded, founding the Hawkshead Nursing Association which brought a District Nurse into the area. She gave a cottage to the village and organised a sale of work to raise funds. Her books were among the objects for sale. "They cost about 3s.6d at the time." A Hawkshead woman who bought an autographed copy laments that her children scribbled in the book, almost obliterating the autograph. "We didn't appreciate her."

Though she did not often visit the local school, she gave to the school one of the John Peel musical jugs, asking that it should be used as a sports trophy. Beatrix was not overtly religious. She had been brought up Unitarian and did not support the church at Far Sawrey. She would sometimes attend the Quaker Meeting House at Colthouse, near Hawkshead, and (as Tom Storey, her long-time shepherd, used to say) when she was visiting her farm at the head of the Troutbeck valley, she might pop into the little church to "be on her own."

My interest in Beatrix Potter began over forty years ago with a chance remark - "I remember Beatrix Potter" - by Mrs Richards, the former Miss Annie Black of Sawrey. She recalled the real Beatrix, not the romanticised figure - one who trudged through the quiet village with rounded shoulders, silky white hair and a face that remained fresh-looking to the end. Beatrix had brilliant blue eyes. Mrs Richards, who remembered the clothes of homespun Herdwick wool, added some minor details - two huge patch pockets at the sides and an old straw hat held firmly to her head by black tape tied under her chin. Her dress came down to her ankles, revealing an inch or two of worsted stockings which were "a kind of heather mixture."

What surprised me, as I conversed with Mrs Richards, was the fact that children feared her, probably because she looked so strange. Young people flattened themselves against the walls as she went by and, when she had passed, they ran away as fast as they could. This was the Beatrix of later years, when she dressed oddly and could be a little testy. Tom Storey, her shepherd, remarked: "If she was that side out, she had no room for children." Josephina Banner told me: "She was lovable. And you must believe that because children loved her right from when she was very young and she went to see the Warne children. And children loved her through her books because they met her there." The Beatrix of Josephina's recollection was radiant and jolly. "She had beautiful, silvery-white hair, very rosy cheeks, beautifully blue young eyes, a lovely smile and when she was very round and fat, and when she was laughing, she would rock backwards and forwards on her chair and slap her little knees."

Buttermere

In 1955, when I made my first special excursion to the Beatrix Potter Country to chat with those who knew her, there was a charm about the Lake District which no longer exists. A high proportion of native folk occupied the quiet little villages. The roads appeared to have only just outgrown their old status as country lanes and they carried little traffic. In those days before the farming revolution, which led to much ploughing and re-seeding and a tediously green landscape, summer was enlivened by fields half full of wild flowers. Beatrix lived at a time when the pace of life was slow. There was a big difference between the Sandys family of Graythwaite and a cottager at Sawrey, but people were then contented with their lot.

Long years ago, I crossed Windermere on what was then a new ferry-boat, Drake, and trudged up Ferry Hill, entering an area of rounded hills rather than of craggy mountains; of woods, reed-fringed lakes and tarns; of field walls made without mortar and farmhouse walls liberally white-washed. Beatrix's water-colours fix Sawrey and its district as it was in calmer times. She kept herself busy, judging sheep at agricultural shows and sitting on committees. One group was concerned with the preserva-tion of footpaths. She and Willie Heelis did not flaunt their wealth; they lived simply, invariably going their own ways, not getting under each other's feet. Margaret Lane wrote in *A Tale of Beatrix Potter* of "law books and papers and deed-boxes at one end of the dining-room, bram-ble jelly and toasted teacakes at the other. There were no tiresome con-cessions to appearance."

To hear first-hand accounts of this remarkable woman has been, for me, a joyful experience. Mrs Richards may have been frightened of her as a child and she certainly thought of Beatrix as being strange, but she respected her for what happened on the day that Mrs Richards' father, Dick Black, died. Beatrix arrived at the house and asked if she could see him. "I took her upstairs; when I turned the sheet back from my dead father's face, she knelt down and wept. 'I've always respected you', she said. 'God bless you'. I was never so near to tears." In later years, Mrs Gaddum, who lived at Braban House, Burneside, told Mary Burkett that Beatrix had a dry sense of humour. She was also by nature a retiring person. "She did not like people coming up to her, fussing, asking for her autograph and saying nice things about her books."

Beatrix was spirited. Dr J N Warren recalled for me when his family lived on the eastern shore of Windermere, directly opposite Sawrey. "About twice a week, Miss Potter would row across and moor her boat at our little pier, then walk the two and a-half miles to Bowness for shop-ping. I was then about six years old and I remember her as a dowdily dressed, kindly lady with a weather-beaten complexion. She took a fancy to my young brother and would often stop to chat with him in his pram. One day she presented him with some beautifully embroidered 'Peter Rabbit' slippers, fashioned by her own hands. Miss Potter subsequently married Mr Heelis, a solicitor whose nephew went to my school. One Sunday, I was his guest at the country house of the 'formidable' Colonel Potter. (When the Colonel let us boys loose in his strawberry bed, I reckoned the epithet most unjustified!). What a pity those slippers were not preserved!"

I first met Tom Storey in 1955. He had arrived at Sawrey from Troutbeck. Beatrix's days as a writer and artist were not over and she gave him the first copy of her *Fairy Caravan*. She liked the look of Herdwick sheep and was a keen supporter of the Breeders' Association established by a family friend, Canon Rawnsley. She took Tom to meetings. They travelled in her chauffeur-driven Wolseley car, "a sit-up-and-beg." She told him of a desire to portray a lamb and asked Tom to let her have the head of the next lamb to die. Tom did so. She fastened the head against a wall and sat on a copy stool in a field to paint it. Tom was amused by much that was said and written. He recognised her great interest in the Herdwick breed of sheep, and he recalled when she was asked to judge sheep at Keswick Show, but, as Tom said: "You can't expect a lady to come out of London and know anything about Herdwick sheep - or any other sheep."

I recall with special clarity my last meeting with Tom. Arriving at his cottage home in Sawrey, I rapped my knuckle against the door and listened for his ever-bright "Come in." This time, the response was delayed. There was time to glance through the window, and to notice that his favourite chair was empty, before I heard his voice faintly inviting me to enter. Tom lay in bed, suffering from an old chest complaint. A few weeks before, he had told me of his impending ninetieth birthday. I now asked him about it. "It's today," he announced. We celebrated, Tom and I, with glasses of sherry. We chatted for a while.

Members of his family were expected, doubtless bringing with them gifts and good wishes.

Anthony Benson, of Plumpton Foot, a quiet area not far from Penrith, was for fifteen years the shepherd at Troutbeck Park. He got to know Beatrix well. Anthony left Troutbeck when his daughter's schooldays were over, being concerned about the difficulty she might have in travelling from the remote farm to a place of work. He told me, with mock gravity, that in fifteen years Beatrix had not paid him once. A pause. He added: "She usually paid t'wife, saying that money should go into the home."

Amanda Thistlethwaite, born at Sawrey but for many years a resident of Hawkshead, gave me an insight into Beatrix's life at Sawrey and allowed me to copy photographs, two of which had been "taken" by Beatrix herself. One is a study of Amanda's mother and members of her family, who posed beside a tree at Ees Wyke. Another, the basis of a water-colour in a Beatrix Potter book, was of Mr Postlethwaite. She called him "Possie" to the annoyance of his wife. The Postlethwaites lived near Castle Cottage and so they saw each other almost daily. Father had been

reticent about a photograph being taken, so he turned his back to the camera. Beatrix photographed the back view, and used it to great effect, the setting being the interior of a barn.

Josephina Banner relates that Beatrix toured the Lake District in "an antiquated, strange-looking black car, very much like a taxi, and driven by a very ancient chauffeur." When attending outdoor events she often carried an umbrella which had belonged to Mr Warne, a partner in the publishing firm, to whom she might have been married but for his untimely death. "There are some silly legends about her being a curmudgeon and all that sort of thing. She was no more curmudgeon than, say, any ordinary Yorkshire person talking Yorkshire to another Yorkshire person, in a straightforward way with a sort of humour that they understand but could be misinterpreted by others." (Beatrix wrote many letters to Josephina, who eventually handed them to Leslie Linder, the man who "cracked" the code of her journal; he left them to what was then the National Book League, now the Book Trust).

Children undoubtedly found the ageing Beatrix very strange, but Willow Taylor told me that if you were able to converse with her at her level, she was at ease with you. "Once, when I was in my teens at Kelsick School, Ambleside, I wanted to borrow a spinning wheel. We were staging scenes from *Cranford*. I called at Castle Cottage and was invited inside. She sat in her favourite rocking chair and wanted to know all about school. And she was only too willing to lend me the spinning wheel for the play." It was Willow who attributed much of the popularity of Sawrey, and more precisely of Hill Top, to the national publicity afforded by *The Tales of Beatrix Potter,* a film of a splendid ballet which, in the early 1970s, turned a trickle of pilgrims into a torrent. Among those pilgrims have been a host of Americans, for whom Beatrix had a special regard. She allowed some of her books to be published in America and not in this country.

Through the Years

1863 (August 8): Rupert Potter, aged 31, marries Helen Leech, aged 24, in the Unitarian chapel at Hyde, near Manchester. Each inherited family fortunes made through the Lancashire cotton industry. Rupert, though called to the Bar, has no financial need to practice.

1866 (July 28): Birth of Helen Beatrix to Helen Potter at No 2 Bolton Gardens, London. Her childhood is attended by loneliness and boredom and she has to find her own amusements. (She becomes an accomplished artist).

1868: Birth of William Heelis, the youngest of eleven children of the Rev John Heelis and his wife Esther.

1871: Rupert, who has been elected a member of the Photographic Society of London, and his wife, a talented artist, find fulfilment in their hobbies during a protracted summer holiday at Dalguise House, near Dunkeld. Young Beatrix is fascinated by the rich and varied wildlife of the district. (Her childhood nurse, a native of the Highlands, had spoken excitedly about witches and fairies).

1872: Birth of Walter Bertram, a brother for Beatrix.

1882: Mr and Mrs Rupert Potter, discovering that Dalguise House in Scotland is unavailable this year, rent Wray Castle for a long holiday. (The Victorian pseudo-baronial mansion on the west shore of Windermere was built in 1848 by Dr Dawson, a wine shipper from Liverpool). Rupert photographs the "castle's" stern exterior, and Beatrix (aged 16) spends part of the holiday sketching and producing water-colours. Family outings include some boating on Windermere. The Vicar of Wray, Hardwicke Rawnsley, drops in to see them frequently and impresses them by his energy, charm and erudition.

1883: Hardwicke Rawnsley becomes Vicar of Crosthwaite, Keswick. His friendship and that of his wife, Eleanor, with the Potters is sustained when they occasionally stay at nearby Lingholm, by Derwentwater.

1885: The Potters rent for a holiday Larkfield Villa, Ambleside. (They are driven up Great Langdale. Beatrix, now a dark and alert little beauty, with hair swept back and dresses at ankle length, is much impressed by Dungeon Ghyll).

1886: A holiday in the Ambleside district is based on Low Wood Hotel. (Beatrix confides in her journal: "Do not care for the Peaks, a poor starved country, extraordinary number of dead sheep").

1887 (September): The Potters are at Lingholm, overlooking Derwentwater and Skiddaw. (About this time, Beatrix is suffering from the effects of rheumatic fever. Ill health had affected her badly in the spring, when she had been taken to Grange-over-Sands).

1889: The Potters tarry at Holehird, Windermere. Beatrix receives instruction in the skills of driving a pony carriage; she finds much pleasure in touring the country lanes.

1891: Sketches submitted by Beatrix Potter to London publishers are rejected. Frederick Warne expressed pleasure at the designs.

1892: The Potters spend their summer holiday in Scotland. (Beatrix begins to form a good collection of fossils).

1893 (September 4th): Beatrix, during a family holiday in Scotland, posts a picture letter featuring a rabbit called Peter to Noel Moore, the first child of Beatrix's favourite governess, who at the age of five is afflicted by a long illness. The letter begins: "I don't know what to write to you, so I shall tell you a story about four little rabbits whose names were - Flopsy, Mopsy, Cottontail and Peter..."

1895 (August): The Potters have a summer holiday at Holehird, beside the road from Windermere to Kirkstone Pass. Beatrix watches hound-trailing at Ambleside Sports, collects fossils in the Troutbeck area, gathers fungi in the grounds of Storrs Hall and is warned by a wood-cutter that "them aren't mushrooms." (On another excursion, Beatrix is "very much struck with the ideal beauty of Coniston...in my opinion far the most beautiful of the larger Lakes").

1895: The Rev H D Rawnsley (with Miss Octavia Hill and Sir Robert Hunter) forms a National Trust and becomes its first honorary secretary. Rupert Potter becomes the first Life Member. Rawnsley, a great friend of the Potters since the days when he was Vicar of Wray, is a classical scholar, an admirer of John Ruskin and a man who writes copiously about Lakeland life and affairs. His wife, Edith, is a keen amateur artist who recognises Beatrix's talent as a water-colourist.

1896: The Potters rent Lakefield, Sawrey, for a long summer holiday. (The house is now called Ees Wyke, or "house on the shore"). Rain falls steadily. Beatrix goes on a fungus-foray. At Hawkshead, she watches the passage of vans hauled by elephants and camels - part of the procession at the arrival of Bostock and Wombwell's Menagerie. Attending worship at the Friends' Meeting House at Colthouse, she is impressed by its old-fashionedness and by the enormous door key. A detraction is a small boy who, when not sucking sweets, is - sighing!

1899: Hardwicke Rawnsley establishes the Herdwick Sheepbreeders' Association. Willie Heelis is admitted as a solicitor, and practises at Hawkshead, where - having come from the Eden Valley - he is known as Appleby Willie.

1900: Willie and Edith Gaddum, cousins of Beatrix, build Brockhole, a mansion set in capacious grounds on the eastern shore of Windermere. They employ Mr Mawson to landscape the gardens.

1900: Hardwicke Rawnsley, asked by Beatrix for advice on the publication of her first book, *The Tale of Peter Rabbit,* does his best to interest London publishers and seeks to improve its chances of acceptance by turning the text into verse.

1901 (December 16th): Beatrix, aged thirty-five, borrows back from Noel Moore the Peter Rabbit letter. She re-writes the story, re-draws the pictures and herself publishes *The Tale of Peter Rabbit* (black and white edition of 250 copies, printed privately). Peter, Beatrix's pet rabbit, dies "at the end of his 9th year".

1902: Frederick Warne publish their edition of *The Tale of Peter Rabbit,* having been instructed by Beatrix that "it was written to a child - not made to order...It must be small enough for very young children to handle and above all it must be cheap...All my little friends happen to be shilling people." The first printing of 8,000 copies (paperback, a shilling; cloth cover, one and sixpence) is covered by advance orders from the book trade. Beatrix herself prints *The Tailor of Gloucester* privately in an edition of 500 copies.

1903: The Potters spend their summer holiday at Fawe Park, Derwentwater. Beatrix makes her first Lakeland purchase, which is a field at Near Sawrey. Warnes re-issue *The Tale of Squirrel Nutkin* and *The Tailor of Gloucester.*

1904: Beatrix sketches in the Newlands Valley, near Keswick, for a new book, *The Tale of Mrs Tiggy-Winkle.* Publication of *The Tale of Benjamin Bunny* and *The Tale of Two Bad Mice.*

1905: Beatrix is engaged to Norman Dalziel Warne, of the publishing family. A shy man, he proposes by letter. Beatrix's parents are displeased at the prospect of her marrying "into the trade". (Norman dies suddenly, on August 25, aged 37, of pernicious anaemia. Beatrix is later to describe him as "a saint, if ever a man was good").

1905: Beatrix buys Hill Top, Sawrey, using royalties from her books with the addition of a small legacy. She tells her over-protective parents that Hill Top, a seventeenth century farmhouse with a modest amount of land, is just an investment. It was to be an escape from London, to be used initially as a holiday retreat. She joyously attends sales to purchase old oak furniture for its rooms. Appearance of *The Tale of Mrs Tiggy-Winkle* and *The Pie and the Patty-pan.*

1906: Hill Top, Sawrey, which she describes as "an old, old house, full of cupboards and passages", is extended to provide accommodation for Mr Cannon, her farm man, and his family. Beatrix does much of her writing in the New Room, which is part of the extension. She delights in being at Hill Top, from which there are views across country of the Coniston and Langdale fells. Publication of *The Tale of Mr Jeremy Fisher.*

1907: Warnes publish *The Tale of Tom Kitten,* a book set in Sawrey, with views of Hill Top and its garden. Beatrix notes that the hall of Hill Top has been "got straight". The furniture and fitments include some old-fashioned chairs and a warming pan which had belonged to her grandmother.

1908: Publication of *The Tale of Jemima Puddle-duck* (written for Ralph and Betsy, the children of John Cannon, manager of Hill Top Farm) and *The Tale of Samuel Whiskers* (written about 1905 and set at Hill Top).

1909: Beatrix buys Castle Farm at Sawrey. She converts the farmhouse, adds the fields to Hill Top and buys Moss Eccles Tarn, planting it with waterlilies and stocking it with fish. Publication of *The Tale of Flopsy Bunnies* (set in Wales) and *Ginger and Pickles.* Hardwick Rawnsley becomes a Canon of Carlisle.

1910: *The Tale of Mrs Tittlemouse* is published. Beatrix campaigns with vigour for tariff reform in the period before a general election. To her dismay, the Liberal Government is returned.

1911: Publication of *The Tale of Timmy Tiptoes* and *Peter Rabbit's Painting Book.*

1912: Willie Heelis proposes marriage to Beatrix, who quietly welcomes it, though it is initially opposed by her elderly parents. Beatrix is

shocked when a flying boat touches down on the once quiet Windermere. She describes the machine as "a beastly fly-swimming spluttering aeroplane."

1913 (summer): Rupert Potter having been seriously ill, a Lakeland holiday is prescribed. Beatrix and her parents summer at Lindeth How in Windermere. Bertram shocks his parents by revealing to them that he has been married for eleven years to Mary, a former maid and daughter of a publican at Hawick. Rupert and his wife withdraw their objection to Beatrix marrying Willie Heelis, and in October, this is solemnised at St Mary Abbot's in Kensington, London. She is 47 and Willie 42, "very quiet - dreadfully shy, but I'm sure he will be more comfortable married." The honeymoon is spent at Sawrey. They take up residence at Castle Cottage. Writing to a niece, Beatrix reports that Uncle Willie has been fishing - "or poaching" - at Moss Eccles Tarn. Warnes publish *The Tale of Pigling Bland*.

1914: Beatrix pays several visits to London to attend to her ailing father. Rupert Potter dies of cancer on May 8. Mrs Potter is ensconsed at Sawrey. The Great War begins. Young men slip away from trades and the farms, don khaki and take their chance on the battlegrounds of France.

1917: Death of Eleanor Rawnsley. Beatrix sends a letter of condolence to Canon Rawnsley (who ere long re-marries, his second bride being Eleanor Simpson).

1918: Willie receives his calling-up papers but is pronounced medically unfit for active service. Sudden death of Bertram, aged 46, at his Scottish farm.

1919: Beatrix's widowed mother settles at Lindeth How, Storrs, along with four maids, two gardeners and the coachman who is now a chauffeur. Beatrix is among those who support a charity to maintain a district nurse in the parishes of Sawrey, Hawkshead and Wray.

1920: Death of Canon Rawnsley at his retirement home at Grasmere. Interment in Crosthwaite churchyard, Keswick.

1924: Beatrix buys Troutbeck Park, a large sheep farm, which has a stock of Herdwick sheep. She travels regularly to the farm in a Morris Cowley car, driven by Walter Stevens, who had been her mother's footman.

1926: Beatrix appoints Tom Storey as her shepherd. With his help, the best of the Herdwicks at Troutbeck Park and Hill Top win awards at Lakeland sheep shows. The sheep-mark for each stock is a letter H (for Heelis).

1929: *The Fairy Caravan* is published in America.

1930: Beatrix buys the 3,000-acre Monk Coniston Estate, which includes Tarn Hows, Tom Heights, Tilberthwaite, Yewdale and the summit of Wetherlam. (This area was once part of the vast estate of Fountains Abbey, in Yorkshire). Beatrix, not having funds for the entire purchase price, offers two-thirds of Monk Coniston to the National Trust at cost price (which is soon covered by receipts from a public appeal). At show time, she sometimes refers to her prize-winning Herdwicks as "our pretty little baas." It is a time of industrial depression. Prices for sheep at the autumn sales are poor. The wool clip at Hill Top is not sold immediately.

1932 (December 20): Death of Helen Potter, the mother of Beatrix, aged ninety-three. Beatrix is somewhat relieved, for visiting mother had involved a ferry crossing of Windermere, and mother was not always inclined to see her. Beatrix once commented in a letter: "My mother is refusing to die." Another time, after being unconscious for four hours, mother had suddenly sat up and asked for tea. Mrs Potter is interred near her old family home in Lancashire.

1934: Beatrix gives many of her water-colours and drawings of fungi, mosses and fossils, also catalogues for the shows she had attended, to the Armitt Library in Ambleside. (Beatrix had become a member on her marriage to Willie Heelis in 1913, he having been the solicitor for the library since it was established in 1912).

1935: Delmar Banner and his wife Josephina (artist and sculptress respectively) settle at a farm in Little Langdale.

1938: Delmar Banner paints a celebrated portrait of Beatrix with a backdrop of a Lake District sheep show. (The original portrait hangs in the National Portrait Gallery in London).

1939: Beatrix enters a Liverpool hospital for a serious operation. She constantly thinks of the welfare of Willie and writes to the two maiden ladies who lived next door to Castle Cottage about what might be arranged if she "went under."

1939: Beatrix welcomes to Sawrey her cousin, Sir William Hyde Parker, of Melford Hall. He, his Danish wife Ulla and their children, have been rendered homeless by the war. They are allowed to live in Hill Top. Sir William, a great angler, joins Willie Heelis at Moss Eccles Tarn.

1940: No 2 Bolton Gardens, Beatrix's "unloved birthplace," is destroyed by bombs.

1943: Beatrix Potter writes to Warne's, her publishers, requesting more copies of her books, having disposed of her stock as prizes to a visiting party of Girl Guides.

1943: Beatrix dies at Castle Cottage on December 22. She is cremated at Blackpool. The death notice requests: "No mourning, no flowers and no letters please." In her will, she stipulates that Hill Top and much else are to become the property of the National Trust. (Beatrix had been invited to become President of the Herdwick Sheepbreeders' Association but died before the appointment was ratified).

1946: Death of Willie Heelis, aged 77. *The Westmorland Gazette* notes his interest in everything locally. "Although reserved, he was a very shrewd man, with a kindly manner. He will be remembered with affection."

1964: Hill Top, Sawrey, is opened to the public by the National Trust.

1966: Death of Captain Duke, a relative of Beatrix, who had occupied her old home, Castle Cottage, for many years.

1966: Centenary of the birth of Beatrix Potter. Leslie Linder publishes his transcript of the 200,000 or so words of Beatrix's journal, which she had meticulously kept from the age of thirteen to thirty. The journal entries reveal her acute powers of observation and her ability, succinctly, to sum up people and experiences.

1971: Filming of *The Tale of Beatrix Potter,* a ballet choreographed by Sir Frederick Ashton.

1973: Leslie Linder and Enid, his sister, leave over 2,000 items of Beatrix Potter interest to the Victoria and Albert Museum as part of the National Art Library.

1976: The Patterson family salvage Beatrix and Willie's flat-bottomed boat from the bed of Moss Eccles Tarn. (It is now an exhibit at the Bowness Steamboat Museum).

1980: Foundation of The Beatrix Potter Society, which seeks to promote the study and appreciation of her life and works.

1986: Death, aged ninety, of Tom Storey, Beatrix's faithful shepherd.

1988: The Beatrix Potter Gallery is opened at Hawkshead in the offices used by the firm of solicitors of which Willie Heelis was a partner.

At Home in Sawrey

BEATRIX POTTER fell in love with Near Sawrey, a Lakeland village which takes its name through its proximity to Hawkshead. The road from Hawkshead passes Esthwaite Water and continues through Near Sawrey, then Far Sawrey, to the Windermere ferry. In Beatrix's day this was steam-driven, operating along two cables, stretched from the Lancashire shore at Ferry Hotel to the eastern or Westmorland shore at the Nab, just south of Bowness.

Sawrey is a cluster of houses, built of native stone, and whitened over to give a summer gleam. The Silurian countryside undulates gently, with tracts of woodland and tarns which are first seen with surprise and delight. The woods still hold a small population of red deer, part of the old Furness stock, the finest free-ranging deer in England. The fields which now have numbers on the map were known for their apt names, including Bull Banks, a pasture on Castle Farm where, by courtesy of Beatrix, the local folk gathered in the 1930s to celebrate the Coronation of George V. Esthwaite Water, being shallow, was quick to freeze over in a prolonged cold snap and became a giant ice rink for local skaters.

At Easter, before the 1914-18 war, Jolly Boys (Pace Eggers) went on their rounds. Basically drama, it was a folk ritual going back to pagan times and dealing with the triumph of summer over winter. In 1912, Beatrix was standing with her camera to record the gavortings of a group of five boys who, in the guise of characters such as Lord Nelson, The Doctor, Bessy Brown Bags and Tosspot, went from house to house, singing the pace-egging song, which ended:

> Now ladies and gentleman who sit by the fire,
> Put your hands in your pockets, it's all our desire -
> Put your hands in your pockets and pull out your purse;
> Come give us a trifle, you'll not be much worse.
> For the diddle dum day, for the diddle de dum day.

The pagan element was Christianised by the substitution of St George slaying the Dragon. Later, the hero became Lord Nelson. The pace-egging play was not merely slapstick comedy but a fragment of man's earliest dramatisation of his religious beliefs. Arthur Raistrick has called it "a fossil from the mind of earliest man." It was the sort of local custom which appealed to Beatrix, as did the decorating of the "pace" eggs themselves, which were hard-boiled and dyed using a time-honoured method involving onion skins or cochineal. The eggs featured in rolling races which took place on a steep hillside on Easter Monday. A traditional dish of this season was Easterledge pudding, made from bistort, which grew in the locality and might also be boiled and consumed as a vegetable.

At Christmas, *The Sawrey Carol,* an unaccompanied hymn, was rendered by the church choir on its festive season rounds of the village; the carollers being invited by the owners of the larger houses to partake of mince pies, the adults being served with mulled ale. Sawrey had its own special carol, which was also sung in church. Ethel Byers, who was dairymaid for Beatrix at Castle Cottage, remembers the words cutting cleanly through the frosty air, under a starlit sky:

> *Hark, hark, when news the angels bring;*
> > *glad tidings of a new-born King;*
> *Born of a maiden virgin pure;*
> > *born without sin (bass singers),*
> > *born without sin from guilt secure (all).*

(Prior to Christmas, 1943, the carol singers were requested not to visit Castle Cottage as Mrs Heelis was very poorly, having been in hospital in Liverpool).

At Near Sawrey, the Tower Bank Arms commands attention because of its whimsical style and a king-sized clock on the porch. The big house, now called Ees Wyke, but formerly known as Lakefield, was rented by the Potter family for a long stay in 1896. Beatrix painted some of its features, also an oak tree in the field sloping down to the lake. Buckle Yeat, now a well-known guest house, was a cottage owned by Bruce Dixon who had a large woodyard. To celebrate the end of the 1939-45 war, children piled on to the back of one of Bruce Dixon's lorries, which was bedecked with red, white and blue, and were taken for a joy ride around Windermere.

Near Sawrey was a thoroughly rural village, with three main farms - Hill Top, of course; also High Green Gate, run by Billy Postlethwaite, and Esthwaite How, the Graythwaite estate. Children used the dusty main road as a playground. "We played rounders," recalls Amanda Thistlethwaite, who as a child regularly met and sometimes had a brief chat with Beatrix Potter. "Sawrey was a lovely unspoilt little village then." Mr Burns was "mine host" at The Tower Arms and Fred Satterthwaite presided over the smithy. Children stared with drooping lower jaws at two ladies who sported bushy beards. They were Mrs Taylor at the shop and Mrs Chapman, wife of a woodman, who seemed to spend half her life standing in the doorway of her house, taking in the sights. She was avoided by children because of her propensity to hug and kiss them.

Presiding over the post office, which stood beside the lane passing Castle Cottage, was Lizzie May, her husband George Garnett and their mother, who is recalled as looking like a witch, being a terrifying sight to a small child who met her in the gloomy passage leading to the room in which post office matters were conducted. Lizzie May herself was a cheerful individual. She and her mother died on the same day and were buried at a double funeral - a "first" for Sawrey.

Churchgoing was not part of Beatrix's routine. She had been reared a Unitarian and if she felt inclined to worship it was in the contemplative quietness of the Quaker Meeting House at Colthouse. When her mother was living at Lindeth Howe, Beatrix would go to church at Troutbeck. Only after her marriage in 1913 did Beatrix live full-time at Sawrey, among "such nice old-fashioned people." Another time she mentioned the "very pretty hill country, but not wild like Keswick or Ullswater."

Willie and Beatrix settled down to married life at Castle Cottage, which Beatrix had selected partly because she did not think Willie would like the clatter of the farmyard and because it was quieter than Hill Top. The view from Castle Cottage was pastoral. A small hill covered with rocks and trees held the bank in which Mr Tod, the fox, had one of his homes. The so-called Cottage was in fact two cottages knocked into one and extended, with a large bay window from which she could scan the whole village. A back staircase was available to her if someone called at the main door and, not wishing to meet them, she retreated up the lane. She liked the garden lush and weedy.

Beatrix cherished the obscurity of her residence, not because she disliked people but so that she would not be over-troubled with visitors. She did not mind an artist living nearby. William H Waddington became a tenant in 1916 and lived close enough to Beatrix to be able to see her almost every day. He told me: "When I first approached Beatrix about accommodation, I was received in a most kindly way. 'I think I would rather like to have an artist living next door', Beatrix said, adding that 'he would not have a gramophone going in the garden. . .'." She began to enumerate many other things which she did not believe a self-respecting artist would do, concluding: "I am quite sure that you, as an artist, would agree with me." Waddington replied: "As a matter of fact, where I have been, I could have wished to have seen far less of my landlord, so this will suit me very well."

Josephina Banner recalls that on her first visit to this house, she and her husband had to go through the gardens of two other houses to reach it. Later, they became acquainted with a backdoor, which gave access to the back lane. Castle Cottage was kept somewhat primitive because Beatrix preferred it that way and, let it be whispered, she was something of a skinflint. At the edge o' dark in winter, a candle sufficed. Then a paraffin lamp would be lit. Not for two years after the arrival of electricity at Sawrey was a connection provided for Castle Cottage, the biggish house at the end of a drive, where Beatrix had her home. She did not take part in the celebrations at the big barn at the Sawrey Hotel to celebrate the coming of electricity to Sawrey in 1933.

Hill Top has never been connected to the electricity grid. Perversely, Beatrix did not object to an electricity supply being installed in the shippon, for perhaps the cows would like it. No telephone wires extended to Castle Cottage. There was a perfectly good public telephone at the post office, a little way along the lane. Beatrix used it to maintain regular contact with her mother, who was frequently ailing and needed her daughter's sympathy if not actual help.

Anyone who saw the interior of Castle Cottage at this time was privileged. Beatrix Potter could be off-putting. As Josephina Banner explained: "She had to say 'no' to some people otherwise her life would have been flooded with visitors wanting her to sign books. She would have had no private life of her own." The first time Josephina and Delmar met Beatrix at her home, they walked round by the back. "There wasn't any proper sort of front door, I think. It was just a door with no knocker. We waited. It was a long wait. We felt it was just like knocking on the door of a shy animal. There were little footsteps. Clogs on the stone floor inside. They went up to the door and waited. Just like a little animal sniffing to see who it was. Then she opened the door a crack. Then she saw who it was and opened it a bit more. 'Cum in'. She was wearing on her head a knitted tea-cosy, with a hole for the spout and a hole for the handle. It was a shade of blue. You can't do better than that, can you?"

Beatrix did not shake hands with her visitors. "She turned and toddled off. We just followed her. Delmar shut the door behind us. We found ourselves in a flagged hall. There was no mat. Two beautiful old guns, with silver mountings, adorned a beam. Then, on the right, a door led into this lovely old room. It was not over-furnished. There was a fireplace, with two easy chairs, comfortable in Victorian red velvet. I remember an old-fashioned dining table. We saw some chocolate wrappers - what Delmar later declared was 'a naughty amount of chocolate paper'. Some straight-backed chairs were available and the visitors sat on these. We sat, rather politely, because Beatrix was awe-inspiring as well as being sweetly pretty." She began to ask questions. "As we answered, and she discovered that we knew the Lakes intimately, she began to open up and became very friendly. She said something very funny. I laughed, and as I laughed I snorted. My husband said: 'Oh, Pig-wig'. It was a nickname that made Beatrix laugh. She very often used this name when she wrote to me."

Josephina has such a clear recollection of that first visit to Castle Cottage that she can recall fine details of a Girton painting that hung there. "It was so suitable - a shepherd, sheep and an approaching storm." Beatrix cherished her own original paintings, each measuring about twelve inches by eight inches. Wrapped in brown paper, with a blue ribbon, they were left behind the geyser in the bathroom at Castle Cottage. "Even in this matter, she was completely original."

Amanda recalls the austere appearance of rooms at Castle Cottage. In the kitchen, there was nothing smart, "just bare flags, a scrubbed table and ordinary ladder-backed chairs. Yet, everything was beautiful and clean. Hams were hanging in the pantry." From the kitchen, a visitor might walk down a passage into what was called the lounge. "I don't think she had a fitted carpet, just a carpet in the middle of the room, as people did in those days." Amanda recalls a piano, a settee and some easy chairs. One or two small tables stood about. From the lounge one might go on to a kind of verandah. "It looked on to the garden. She had an extension made to provide a big bedroom; it had lovely bay windows."

The menu at Castle Cottage could be simple. A visitor for tea in the 1930s saw a green tablecloth with bobbles. Tea consisted of bread and butter, with no cake. Another visitor sat down to a plate of cold mutton and noted that only one half of the dining table had been cleared for the meal. The other half was cluttered with papers. Conversely, when Josephine and Delmar Banner visited her there was "plenty on the table and she herself had two helpings of everything." She did not dominate the conversation, being interested in all that Delmar had to say.

Mrs M R Ormerod, of Reading, writing to the *Radio Times* in 1971, recalled going to live in Sawrey in 1919. In the following year, Beatrix asked Mrs Ormerod if she would employ a Sawrey girl in whom she was interested. This she was glad to do. "After that, she invited our elder son, aged six, and me to tea in her cottage. He was well read in her books, and they got on well together. I remember that he asked her if she would write a story about our goats, but she said that she would write no more stories as her eyesight was not good enough for her to do the illustrations."

Beatrix gave the Ormerod children two hard-boiled Easter eggs painted by herself. "One showed the head of a child with golden curls and blue eyes, and the other the head of an old man with bald head and side whiskers. I kept the eggs for many years in a display cabinet. When we regretfully had to leave Sawrey to live in a town, she kindly volunteered to take over our children's pet rabbits. They had a great deal of freedom with us, and we were afraid that a new owner might shut them in boxes."

When she was writing, Beatrix scarcely spoke for days on end. Mrs Rogerson, her housekeeper, knew when it was wise to speak to her or not. At other times, her company was pleasant. The Postlethwaites of High Green Gate were near neighbours of the Heelises of Castle Cottage - so close, indeed, that there could be territorial disputes. The geese belonging to the Postlethwaites found their way into Beatrix's garden and began to crop the lawn. Amanda recalls: "Mrs Heelis came to our door and said to my mother: 'Will you tell Possie Amanda's father to get his geese off my land. They're eating all my grass'. She was very bitter about anything like that."

About a fortnight later, Beatrix's turkeys were on the Postlethwaite land. Amanda relates: "Now my mother was one of the sweetest women you could ever wish to meet. (She used to tell my father to stop arguing with Beatrix, for they often discussed farming and he knew he was wrong. He argued simply to make her annoyed). When the turkeys were on our land, my mother saw red, for hadn't Beatrix told her off about our geese? Mother walked across to Castle Cottage, went up their drive and knocked at the door. When it had been opened, mother said: 'Mrs Heelis, will you take your turkeys off our land? You wouldn't allow our geese to be on yours'. It wasn't a bit like mother to do this, but the incident of the geese still rankled with her."

Despite their abrasive conversations, Beatrix loved to sit and chat with Mr Postlethwaite. They would sit in the porch at High Green Gate and talk about sheep for hours. Amanda recalls: "After a while, my father would get up in his majesty, and Beatrix would get up in her majesty, and she'd remark: 'Possie, you're not worth talking to'. He'd say: 'No more are you, Mrs Heelis'. She'd say: 'You'd better get yourself on to t'fell where you've nobody to fall out with - that's your best place'. Yet, next day, she was back, talking to him. She never bore any malice."

After leaving school, which was at Far Sawrey, involving children in a mile round-trip twice a day, Amanda worked at High Green Gate for two years. She had lots of encounters with the redoubtable Beatrix. "I used to clean the shippons out, and if she came out of her back gate she would pass the time of day and say: 'Are you working again, Amanda?' Or something like that." Amanda had, in fact, milked cows from being nine years old. "We had ten cows, though I wouldn't milk ten at any one time. We had pigs and sheep - Herdwicks and Swaledales."

At Castle Cottage, two widows - Mrs Benson and Mrs Rogerson - did the housework and the cooking. They did not "live in", having cottages in the village. Tommy Christopherson attended to the garden, Tommy Willan was the handy man and a small orchard at the back of the house was left to look after itself. Tom Storey, who called daily with milk, told me: "Mrs Heelis was always up and about in good time. You'd hear the clatter of her clogs on the flagged floors."

Anthony Benson, when visiting Castle Cottage, got no further than a chair just inside the kitchen. "That's where you sat, about two paces in. She'd fetch you a cup o' tea, and one meat sandwich, and that was that!" Anthony used to call on his way back to Troutbeck Park Farm after attending to sheep on her other farms. "She would never say - 'I'll take you back'. After your cup o' tea, you'd to walk down to t'ferry, cross Windermere and tramp up Bowness and on to Troutbeck." Anthony added: "There wasn't a day lang enough."

The Tower Bank Arms was seen daily by Beatrix. She entered it only when she wished to report yet another supposedly naughty deed by Willow, the youngest daughter of William Edward Burns, who was "mine host" for 35 years, ran a taxi - and knew that Beatrix's idea of naughtiness might be nothing more than bouncing a ball. Willie Heelis was well disposed towards children and thought nothing of visiting the Tower Bank Arms, not to prop up the bar and quaff ale from Alexander's Brewery at Kendal but to rehearse folk dance steps with others on the blue-flag floor of the large kitchen, where for the duration of the rehearsal a pegged rug and coconut matting were rolled up.

Mrs Margaret Burns, of the Tower Bank Arms, saw Beatrix every day and told me that they often chatted under an old apple tree. "She was a character. I liked her very much but, mind you, if anyone got on the wrong side of her I don't think they ever got back into her favour again. I used to say nothing - or simply side with her. It was the best way. You could talk to Beatrix Potter and be sure that what she said would be interesting."

My own first insight into what life was like at Sawrey at the time

Beatrix lived there was the conversation I had over four decades ago with Annie Richards (nee Black). Her parents were well-known residents of the village. They eventually moved into a cottage standing in Beatrix Potter's farmyard. The Black family now saw more of Beatrix than they had done before and they began to know her true self. "Behind that quaint dress and bent head there was a very beautiful character. Even my father began to think there was 'nowt much wrang' with her after all. Her many kindnesses she showed towards my parents are too numerous to mention, but this I must tell you."

Annie recalled how there was an orchard adjoining the farmyard. It was well stocked with apples and plum trees. Beatrix Potter came to the cottage of the Black family and said: "Now there are my fruit trees. I don't want you to help yourselves, but I have given you one apple and one plum tree. I've put a red band round each of them. You can have the fruit from those two trees." As Annie pondered about that incident, she saw behind it a great moral. "Beatrix Potter must have thought all

43

that fruit would be a temptation, so to avoid it she offered some of it to the children. It was much nicer to have a tree to pick from than to be given a basketful of fruit." She did not care much for change. Old Mrs Black painted the door of the cottage dark green but, impulsively, decided that two panels should be white. Beatrix was soon on the doorstep demanding that the decoration of the door should be a uniform green.

A person of regular ways, Beatrix passed along the drive below the garden of the house leased by William Waddington and his family. She could be seen on this route every morning at precisely the same time - followed by turkeys, ducks, geese and any other feathered creatures that happened to be near. These were attracted by the hot mash she carried in a bucket. Beatrix had a stick with which she stirred the mash. She beat the bucket and all the time she sang a cadence of song. As a landlord, she could not have been kinder to the Waddingtons. "She made me a big studio in the house by arranging for a wall to be knocked down; she went to considerable expense to make it a comfortable home."

The Post Office which served Near Sawrey was closed and is now Low Green gate, a doubtle-fronted house occupied, at the time of writing, by Edward (Ted) Jackson, whose late wife was Freda, daughter of Tom Storey and custodian for many years of Hill Top. Ted directed me to the remains of a stile now held in a vice-like grip by a hedge, situated just across the lane from his home. The stile was not used during Beatrix's life by anyone other than herself and her employees. The field was a meadow and the grass must not be trampled. This was well-known to Beatrix. She used the postbox which was let into a window. She was familiar with the passage, leading into a room which had a deal counter dividing it into two.

Beatrix eventually came to own the building in which the Post Office once operated. It happened following the deaths of Lizzie May Garnett and her mother. That left brother George, who by himself was not capable of dealing the Post Office affairs. He had run a little business charging wet batteries for local people and repairing cycles. Beatrix bought the handsome house and also an associated barn. The Post Office was closed down (henceforth, the business was conducted at Far Sawrey) and chauffeur Walter Stevens was ensconsed in the house.

Amanda Postlethwaite, who had done farm work for two years, now found a job at the grocery shop owned by the Taylors. "I worked here for four years." Those were the days when provisions arrived in bulk and were cut to size at the time of purchase. Sweets were in tall glass jars. The shopkeeper thought nothing of handling unwrapped sweets and, showing adroitness of a rare order, making a cone from a single piece of paper in which to drop them.

Beatrix was a regular customer at the shop. Amanda served her many a time. "She'd come probably for some sugar, if she'd run short, or for some sweets." When Amanda was to be married and leave the shop, Beatrix came to the door and announced: "Mr Heelis says I've got to give you a present." The shop closed because people tended to buy Jack-o'-the-Pinch, an expression used when they'd run out of anything. Beatrix wrote about this little shop in *Ginger and Pickles*. In her day, the windows had small panes. "You went down this passage and in at the right hand side, and then it had a counter and it wasn't much bigger than the living room of a house. We kept our flour in an oak chest. Herbs and spices were kept in small wooden drawers. It was a lovely little shop. You'd see bacon hanging up and we had to cut lard according to demand..."

Beatrix's dislike of novelty is indicated by a story told by Amanda Thistlethwaite (nee Postlethwaite) who says that after she and her husband were married, they erected a wireless pole to improve reception. "And do you know, we had it up for only two days when Mrs Heelis came up the steps to the house and said to me: 'Amanda, who gave you permission to put that wireless pole up?' I said: 'Our landlord', who was Bob Taylor. I added: 'You only have to ask your landlord, surely'. Beatrix snapped back: 'Well, it's to come down. You can tell Robert he's to take it down'. I said: 'Very well, I'll tell my husband when he comes'."

Robert wrote Beatrix a letter. There was no reply, and in retrospect the Thistlethwaites realised it was a dreadful pole. "It was put up in the days when you thought the higher the pole went, the better was the radio reception."

Treasures at Hill Top

HILL TOP, Sawrey, is superficially very much as it was in Beatrix's day. It was her retreat from an increasingly turbulent world, a place where she might think, paint or take pleasure in her treasures. Tom Storey's wife had foretold what its future might be when she remarked: "Tell you what it is, father, this place will be a museum one day." Tom asked her why she had said this, and she added: "Just go through there and look at the stuff she's bringing in."

Hill Top and the adjacent farmer's quarters were inter-connected. A door led from one kitchen to another. Tom's wife looked after Hill Top in winter and sometimes, going through the door, she'd find Beatrix sitting quietly, painting or just thinking. "When Hill Top started as a museum, folk kept coming into our house through the connecting door, so it was built up."

The large dairy at Hill Top "got no sun at all" and was devoted to the making of butter and cheese. Mrs Cannon took special pride in making butter, exhibiting a sample in the produce tent at Hawkshead Show. Before the Storey family arrived, in the late 1920s, Beatrix had a dairymaid to attend to these matters. Twice a day, the few cows were hand-milked and the cream was separated, to be placed in a crock until it ripened. The butter-making process involved a churn, the turning of which was a tedious task. In summer, an age seemed to go by before the butter formed and the churn began to judder. It was a process which forever fascinated Beatrix, who had no part to play in it except to spread some of the butter on freshly-baked bread.

Josephina Banner recalls the rabbits kept in a hutch in the garden, "so that children would not be too disappointed if they visited the place and could not find Peter Rabbit. 'Children think he lives with me', Beatrix used to say. When they ask: 'Is Peter with you?' I say - 'These are his relations'." In truth, Beatrix had not even seen Hill Top when she wrote *The Tale of Peter Rabbit*. It was penned while holidaymaking in Scotland. The garden of Hill Top is much changed. On the left, as you approached the house, was a vegetable plot, intermingled with flowers. On the other side lay a flower bed with old-fashioned flowers such as delphiniums, hollyhocks, lupins and pansies.

Beatrix had purchased Hill Top with part of the royalties earned for her by *Peter Rabbit* and from a small legacy she received from an aunt. Hill Top was a working farm, complete with cattle, sheep, pigs, clucking hens and quacking ducks. It was tenanted by John Cannon, his wife and two children and when the farmhouse was extended they were given fresh accommodation. John now became a farm manager.

Beatrix retained for her own use the original rooms and took enormous pleasure in furnishing them with objects of local interest and appropriate age. The spirit of her remarkable personality lingers inside the house, where the light brings a responsive gleam from oak beams and panelling. Beatrix's life was so closely associated with the house that as you wander round you half expect to come across her, busy at her needlework or thumbing over the certificates she had won at local shows with her farm stock.

The first people to sleep in Hill Top after Beatrix Potter took up residence at Castle Cottage were her cousin, Sir William Hyde Parker and his family. His residence, Melford Hall, was taken over by the Army at the start of the 1939-45 war. He received serious head injuries while on duty with the Home Guard in the blackout. When he came out of hospital, his cousin Beatie (Beatrix Potter) and the quiet village of Sawrey, so far from the front line, came to mind. She allowed them to move into Hill Top. The transition from Melford Hall to a modest-sized building at Sawrey was profound but much appreciated, for here the health of Sir William improved greatly. Ulla was to relate that coal was kept in the old pig-sty and kindling was picked up from the ground in a local wood.

Susan Ludbrook, who offered to act as custodian at Hill Top for a short trial season, met Beatrix for the first and last time in 1939 and was left with an impression of a person of great delicacy and kindness. As custodian, she was assisted by Freda Storey, the young daughter of Tom, who had always looked after Hill Top for Beatrix and loved the old house. In 1966, while editing *Cumbria* magazine, I persuaded Mrs Ludbrook to recall her Hill Top days for our readers. There was no formal opening in 1946, when a few people with an interest in the National Trust had gathered by personal invitation. The house was subsequently open to villagers, friends and to any who had known Beatrix and wished to pay tribute to her memory.

On the opening day, after discussion, it was decided to open the house for a prescribed period. Visitors would be welcomed and given a tour of the house and garden. No one knew how many people would respond, for the war was not long over, austerity prevailed, members of the Armed

49

forces were returning to their loved ones and petrol was rationed. A trickle of visitors was experienced. After the brutality of war, they were enchanted by the wicket-gate, by the flagged path and the old stone porch and oak door.

They found pleasure in walking round the big farm kitchen and noting its wide chimney and old dresser. They climbed the wide staircase leading to the landing above, to see an oak-framed bed on which naughty kittens had played and, best of all, a treasure-room complete with two fair-haired dolls and doll's house, with everything just as it had been arranged by Beatrix herself.

Ten thousand visitors, one in six of whom were children, arrived in the summer of 1946 and the National Trust decided that in the following year Hill Top would be opened at Easter for a full season. That spring saw the publication of Margaret Lane's book, *The Tale of Beatrix Potter,* which was compiled with the consent of Willie Heelis. The book was also published in America and became a best-seller. Hill Top experienced a rapid increase in the number of visitors. Eventually, around nine thousand adults and over two thousand children were visiting Hill Top each summer, leading to changes in the formerly quiet routine of the village. Only in August, the main holiday month, was there congestion. The motorists and ramblers who arrived were able to have tea, scones and cakes in some of the cottages, the owners of which regaled them with personal memories of Beatrix. So many visitors came from the east that the Windermere ferry was replaced by a larger one.

Susan Ludbrook took special pleasure in making the old brasswork gleam. Freda, who loved the garden and knew Beatrix's taste in flowers, kept the rooms florally colourful. Among the visitors were Margaret Lane, whose book had stimulated interest in Beatrix, and Graham Sutton, the Lakeland novelist. The writer H V Morton spent a day in the house with a photographer preparing an article for the *National Geographical Magazine.* The "Aunties" from the popular BBC

Children's Hour brought a group of children and a broadcast from Hill Top was arranged. Wilfred Pickles invited Freda to join him in a radio broadcast.

In 1951, an unexpected development took place which was to alter the whole future of Hill Top and attract an even wider range of visitors. In May of that year, Leslie Linder paid his first visit, which lasted only three days. Susan recalled: "I soon discovered that under his quiet manner and unassuming approach was a specialised interest in the Beatrix Potter stories, and in her art as applied to children's education." Leslie wished to compile and publish a book to be entitled *The Art of Beatrix Potter,* annotated and made available to students and others interested in this aspect of her creative work. "It was not to be a second biography, as this side had been admirably covered by Margaret Lane, whose *The Tale of Beatrix Potter* had by this time become the standard work on her life. It was to be a companion book, showing Beatrix Potter as an artist in many more fields than her stories, and throwing light on what had become known as 'the Hidden Years'."

Not until the following season, 1952, did Leslie Linder return to Hill Top, staying with Mrs Kenyon in the corner house across from the Tower Bank Arms - the building which, indeed, had been the village shop when Beatrix wrote her story of *Ginger and Pickles.* "It was finally decided to print a limited edition of 5,000 copies of *The Art of Beatrix Potter,* so as to preserve for posterity the creative years of one who had stepped unchallenged into her rightful place among Lakeland writers and artists for her purity and clarity of language, and for the sheer beauty of her animal portraiture in Lakeland settings. The book, published at four guineas, was quickly sold out." Leslie Linder visited Hill Top again in 1957 and, noticing how often his book was being asked for by visitors, and afraid it might be badly damaged, he presented another copy, to be held in reserve. Susan induced this shy and modest man to sign it.

In 1959, the last during which Susan Ludbrook was connected with Hill Top, the sun shone throughout the summer. Leslie Linder spent part of his holiday here again, this time bringing his sister, Enid, and they worked on cataloguing the manuscripts. They were intrigued by one parcel which had never been examined. It turned out to be a bundle of old exercise books with odd leaves interspersed. One on the top was evidently in German. The whole bundle was tied with string. When the book top had been removed, the rest appeared to be in code.

Freda Jackson

Susan Ludbrook related in the article she wrote for *Cumbria* readers in 1966 what has become a familiar story, of how Leslie Linder submitted the code to experts who were skilled in unravelling the usual ones. The few clues from the Beatrix fragment fitted into no known or accepted sequence. He began to despair of ever unlocking the secret. On an Easter evening, he had a last try, at last found a clue and began a patient de-coding, magnifying, arranging and assembly of the material into consecutive narrative. The work was spread over four years in the life of an already busy man and his sister. They travelled to Scotland and other places to photograph scenes she described. They visited art galleries and studied newspapers and available documents of the period. The story of the early "hidden years" was revealed. The publication of the *Journal* in 1966 was the centenary tribute of Leslie Linder and his sister to Beatrix Potter. They had never met her but had loved her through her books and in their personal work among children in Sunday School.

When I first knocked on the door of Hill Top over forty years ago, Freda, who was now Mrs Ted Jackson, gave me a brief glimpse of the rooms and their contents, apologising for the untidiness and dust. Alterations had been carried out. The workmen were not long departed. Beatrix looked down on me from the painting by Delmar Banner, who gave his study of her a backdrop of Keswick showfield. In the house were miniatures of the characters she had created. As Squirrel Nutkin had collected nuts in the autumn, so Beatrix gathered round herself a stock of quaint but beautiful objects.

Freda told me that the house had become, in a sense, a museum a year after Beatrix's death. Among the thousands of visitors was a grand old Australian lady who sat looking at the window ledge for a long time, then remarked: "Isn't it wonderful. They've even kept her vacuum flask." This flask was, indeed, used by Susan Ludbrook. With a sudden influx of visitors, she had had no time to put it out of sight. Freda, who grew up in Sawrey and knew much about Beatrix, told me that her love of animals extended to guinea pigs, white mice and two Pekingese dogs, the latter being "put to sleep" when Beatrix died. Susan Ludbrook's special interest lay with the manuscripts and drawings, which Beatrix had left only partly identified and entirely uncatalogued, though she had inserted slips of paper here and there, indicating her intentions. The partnership with Freda lasted the whole of her thirteen seasons as custodian.

For years until he retired, the gardener at Hill Top was Harry Byers, who had been Beatrix's gardener at Castle Cottage. Harry, who with his wife and daughter lived at Fair Rigg, beside Ferry Hill, was a much-respected man locally, and was for forty years a warden at Sawrey Church. At the time of writing, his wife, Ethel, who was dairymaid for Beatrix, is living at Staveley, aged ninety-six.

As Others Saw Her

BEATRIX was, as Tom Storey recalled in a programme broadcast on Radio Cumbria, "rather quiet, reserved, but good to work for if you went the right way about it." Tom spoke reflectively, with pauses between sentences. "She was a good farmer. She took notice of her men. If she knew she had a good man, she took notice of him. She'd never done any farming. She learnt as she went on. She learnt from her farm men and farmers round about the district. She was one of those people who didn't dress up. She was in the Herdwick Sheep Breeders' Association and used to go to meetings in her clogs." When it was suggested that she looked rather like Mrs Tiggywinkle, the hedgehog, featured in one of her books, Tom replied: "Aye - she was rather stooped."

Even in old age, Beatrix had a fresh complexion and could at times demonstrate a jolly nature. William Waddington, who lived near her, mentioned her "tight little knitted bonnet" under which was a face that had the complexion of a child's. She had lovely rosy cheeks and always looked alive and jolly. Tom Storey mentioned her dark brown, rather frizzy hair and the round face, with "a lovely complexion for an old lady." Her clothes were a matter of comment among those who did not know her well. She always wore a velvet band round her neck.

Amanda Thistlethwaite's first memory of her was of seeing her walk down the road wrapped in sacks. "She had a bit of a hat on. I thought: 'What a funny old woman'. I suppose I was only about six years old at the time. She just walked down the road, looking at everything, grunting with disapproval at this and that..."

When I asked Tom Storey how Beatrix was dressed, he replied: "Not like a lady. She wore an old herringbone costume, the skirt extending down to the ankles, a floppy sort of hat - and clogs on her feet. They were black clogs, with clasps to fasten them." Mrs Birkett, of Elterwater, recalled the sack Beatrix had worn round her shoulders and the old felt hat that had crowned her head. "I was living at Grasmere at the time I first saw her. I was cook-housekeeper to two old ladies, Misses Mary and Laura Bradley. The thing I remember about Beatrix Heelis is that she was a funny old lady with a sack round her shoulders. She wore a trilby hat. A man's trilby hat!"

Beatrix did not dress up especially well for a ride in her chauffeur-driven car. "The chauffeur would let her off and just march about till she returned." A lad who was staying with an uncle and aunt at Meadowcroft recalls having to go to Hill Top each morning for the milk. He watched Beatrix, in old clothes, emerging from a pig sty, and he thought: "Poor thing - she has to sleep with the pigs."

Her clogs were made by Charlie Brown, at Hawkshead. He used "kip" or split leather, beech soles and iron caulkers or "irons". Beatrix had rather small feet; she "didn't take above size four." When attending Hawkshead Show, she made an effort to dress well, but her best clothes were old. Amanda Thistlethwaite says: "You know how a grey tweed goes green with age. Well, this happened with Mrs Heelis. She didn't care about dress. And she didn't seem to care much for anybody who cared about dress!"

Beatrix might look like a farmer's wife, but her voice was cultured and refined, with no trace of a North Country accent, except when mimicing one of the local people, usually in some humorous context. In contrast, as Charlie Brown was fond of recalling, her chauffeur, Walter Stevens, was a Cockney who "tried to talk a bit of his own tongue and a bit of the local dialect." Beatrix hired him after he had been serving a local family, and she bought the family car, a Wolseley, to go with him. Walter "drove at about a snail's pace."

When Beatrix's mother lived at Lindeth Howe, she visited her daughter at Sawrey in a smart carriage and pair, with a coachman and

Beatrix Potter at Eskdale Show
(photo: Victoria and Albert Museum).

Above - Hill Top, Near Sawrey, where Beatrix kept her treasures.
Her residence was Castle Cottage, not far away.

Below - Tom Storey, with son and a prize-winning Herdwick of
Beatrix's stock.

Above - Willie Heelis
(foreground) with folk dancers.

Left - The office at Hawkshead
where Willie Heelis was a
partner in a firm of solicitors.

Above - Edith Gaddum, cousin of
Beatrix, who lived at Brockhole.

Above - The Tower Bank Arms at Near Sawrey.
Below - In the Village of Troutbeck.

Above - Josephina Banner, who with her artist husband,
Delmar, visited Beatrix Potter.
Below - Low Yewdale, on the Monk Coniston estate.

A photograph of Mr Postlethwaite, farmer of Sawrey,
taken by Beatrix Potter. Look carefully and you will see there are
two children in view.

Right - Amanda
Thistlethwaite (nee
Postlethwaite) a native of
Sawrey who regularly met
Beatrix Potter.

Below - Anthony Benson,
shepherd at
Troutbeck Park.

Above - Tom Storey, Beatrix's shepherd at Sawrey, with three cronies, assessing the value of Herdwick sheep.

Below - A fine Herdwick tup.

flunkey. Her mother reminded William Waddington of Queen Victoria. The Waddingtons would watch the carriage and pair being driven to Castle Cottage. When it returned, Beatrix herself would be sitting in it, wearing her old farming attire which constrasted with the smart clothes of her mother. They would be driven to Bowness in the carriage and here Beatrix would do her shopping. Mr Waddington had been told that she would get out of this wonderful carriage and clatter across the causeway into the shops wearing the clogs she had on her feet in the farmyard.

Tom Storey enjoyed his years of being employed by a celebrated land-owner. "She was a good person to work for, but she could be 'funny'. You could meet her at one time, and she'd never look sideways at you. Another time, she'd stop and talk. But she never liked to talk for long." She enjoyed the company of Americans and at times gave the impression she was merely tolerating English folk.

Her manner sometimes caused offence. Tom's wife had been in bed for a fortnight with internal bleeding. She got up and told Tom she would make an effort to feed the hens. "I told her, 'Now don't you go out there. You might not be able to get back'. Those hens were on the far side of the field. She went out, though, and Mrs Heelis saw her feeding the hens. She went out to meet her and didn't even ask my wife how she felt. She just said: 'Oh, you'll soon get over it. It's nothing'. I thought to myself: 'Now, that's done it. She'll never bother with Mrs Heelis again'. And she never did. My wife gave her such a telling-off that day!"

Beatrix bought Dale End at Grasmere. When the only son of the farmer was to be married, she gave the old couple notice, stating that they would never be able to manage without their lad. When she arrived at the farm a little while later, the old lady would not let her in. "She shut the door and bolted it." On the other hand, Beatrix was capable of many kindnesses. Tom told me that she was especially fond of old people. When Old John Taylor was bed-ridden, Beatrix visited him regularly. She asked him what was his favourite animal, and he replied: "A dormouse." She promptly went home and wrote her book about dormice, which she dedicated to the old man.

When Tom was interviewed for Radio Cumbria, he said in response to a question: "She's very little mentioned in the village nowadays." However, a film was being "shot" in the area. The presence of the film-makers was mentioned to Tom. He hadn't been to see a film in the making. "I hadn't time," he said.

Hill Top, Sawrey

Married to Willie Heelis

BEATRIX was shy of people, especially of men, yet when her marriage to William (Willie) Heelis had taken place in 1913, and she had returned to Sawrey from London, she walked down the village carrying a plate on which reposed pieces of wedding cake. The villagers were invited to sample it. "And wish me luck," she added. This story was related to me by William Waddington, one of her tenants. Clara Boyle, of Ambleside, recalled Willie as being "broad and tall. To look at him, he was more like a farmer than a professional man."

In spite of some reluctance on the part of her parents, Beatrix married the quiet, unassuming solicitor who was known to local people as Appleby Willie, from his origins. The Heelis family into which Beatrix married can be traced back to the Craven district of Yorkshire, where in 1652 a yeoman, John Heelis, of Addingham, was given a 99-year lease on land at Skibeden by Lady Anne Clifford. He married a Moorhouse from Skipton. A descendant, Thomas Heelis, became agent to the Earl of Thanet at Skipton Castle, and subsequently at Appleby Castle, where he was also to be remembered as a landowner who became Mayor of the old Westmorland town.

Willie came from a family which produced clerics, doctors, land agents and solicitors. Edward Heelis, his grandfather, was Rector of Long Marton for over forty years. John, a son, was also a clergyman with the good fortune to become Rector of Long Marton, a well-endowed parish in the Eden Valley. He married Esther, a member of the Martin family of Patterdale, and she bore him eleven children. Willie Heelis was one of four brothers, two of whom (like him) became solicitors and two "went into the Church." When Edward Heelis retired from the living of Long Marton, he bought an old coaching inn and converted it into the imposing

Battlebarrow House. It eventually housed Willie's sisters and the young Heelises while they were attending Appleby Grammar School.

The nickname Appleby Willie was a natural one to bestow when, in 1899, as a newly admitted solicitor, he had moved to an old-established firm of solicitors at Hawkshead. An existing partner, William Dickenson, had been dubbed Hawkshead Willie. The newcomer lodged with his two spinster sisters, so at the time he was courting Beatrix his address was the imposing Hawkshead Hall. It was to the Heelis office in the village that Beatrix Potter, on one of her visits to Lakeland from the family home in London, went for legal advice. With increasing affluence, she had began to buy up property and needed a professional to attend to her affairs. There was soon a rapport between them. Willie and Beatrix would meet, sometimes on a Sunday afternoon, to visit properties which she might add to her growing list. When travelling to Sawrey, Willie drove a motor cycle.

Though a handsome man, of moderate height, and fairly slim, Willie had a somewhat colourless manner. The only incident from his childhood which survived as a family story was the time he kept a ferret in his desk. Otherwise, then and in adulthood, he was unsmiling and taciturn. He did have charm, and this seems to have appealed to Beatrix, though was discounted by her parents when the question of marriage was broached. There was a decided difference in social status and, in any case, the Potters had grown accustomed to having Beatrix at their beck and call. They relented when their only son, Bertram, dropped the pro-verbial bombshell and revealed that he had been secretly married for eleven years.

On courting nights, Willie arrived at Sawrey on his fashionable Brad-bury motor bike with a wickerwork sidecar. When the "happy" couple became engaged and a studio photograph was taken, using an ornate chair as the main prop, Beatrix sat on the chair, with the suggestion of a smile, and tight-lipped Willie had balanced himself on one of the chair arms. Beatrix had at least taken the trouble to dress up. Just before the engagement was announced, the wife of Willie's partner in the solicitors' practise had encountered a beshawled, tweed-swaddled figure, clattering along in clogs, and carrying a butter basket containing flowers - a person to whom she was introduced as Beatrix Potter.

With marriage imminent, and Castle Cottage chosen as their future home, Beatrix busied herself with the help of her housekeeper, Mary Rogerson, preparing the place for residence. The alterations had not been completed when Beatrix and Willie were married at St Mary Abbot's Church, Kensington, in the autumn of 1913. Beatrix's parents had the grace to attend the ceremony and they signed the register. A photograph taken that day shows the couple with uncreased faces and wearing the clothes they had donned for the engagement print. This time, Beatrix was standing, her head surmounted by a hat which held a mass of artificial blossom. It was Willie's turn to sit and he did so self-consciously, with crossed arms and crossed legs.

Two days later, a report of the wedding was published in *The Westmorland Gazette* as follows: "In the quietest of quiet manners, two very well-known local inhabitants were married in London on Wednesday. The two parties to this most interesting wedding were Mr W Heelis of Hawkshead Hall and Miss Helen Beatrix Potter of Hill Top, Sawrey. None of their friends knew of the wedding, which was solemnized in the simplest form, characteristic of such modest though accomplished bridegroom and bride. Mr Heelis is the son of the late Rev John Heelis. He comes of one of the most athletic and sporting County families. He himself is one of the best all-round sportsmen in the Lake District. There is hardly a finer shot in the countryside. He is a keen angler. The bride is a successful exhibitor at local agricultural shows of shorthorn cattle and her name is known now all over the country for those charming books for children which have become so deservedly popular."

A short honeymoon in London was followed by a return to Sawrey with, it is related, a white bull calf reposing on the back seat of Willie's car. They had collected the calf at the railway station. It was a stressful time for both. Beatrix had to visit London now and again to attend to her ailing father. Willie made for Appleby, where an old aunt was not so well. Meanwhile, Beatrix was being pestered by her publishers, who wanted another book. At Christmas, Beatrix and Willie joined the Heelis aunties and visiting members of the clan at Battlebarrow House, Appleby. Beatrix bore into the house a Hawkshead Cake, of raisin-speckled pasty, being second cousin of an Eccles Cake.

During the 1914-18 war, Willie served on the War Agricultural Committee; he was also a reserve policeman who refused to wear the obligatory "tin hat". When at home, the two of them shared the cooking and curing of hams. Willie's legal know-how was of assistance to local farmers. He was known to give helpful advice when farmers called at Castle Cottage out of office hours. They appear to have got on well in their married life. Annie Richards told me: "She never interfered with his comings-and-goings." She never forgot to remind anyone who made a mistake, and called her by her maiden name, of her marital status. "She would say: 'I'm not Beatrix Potter any more; I'm Mrs Heelis'."

Willie, who had been sporty since his youth, had a fondness for golf, bowls, billiards, swimming and folk dancing. He was, according to Tom Storey, "a terrible big man on the bowling green" and became president of the Hawkshead club. He also found pleasure in shooting. Tom used to recall: "I never saw such a state Hill Top was in when I came down here from Troutbeck Park. It was over-run with rabbits. Absolutely worried with 'em. A four acre field by t'road was a rabbit warren. One Saturday, Bill Atkinson came to shoot rabbits. I went with him and Mr Heelis after dinner. At t'roadside field, he put a ferret in a hole and bolted 26 rabbits. Willie Heelis shot 'em all. Didn't miss one. He was a great man wi' a gun..."

After the Great War, an enthusiasm for folk dancing swept the Lake

District. Willie took part in ordinary dances, such as *Strip the Willow* and *Rufty Tufty,* and also the more elaborate steps of Morris and sword dancing. Amanda Thistlethwaite recalls dancing in the large kitchen at Hill Top, and adds: "She used to come and watch us dance." Beatrix did not participate and it was said by some people that she had asked him to join the Sawrey dancing group because she did not want the young girls to be left alone with the male teacher at the time. "She was suspicious of everybody." Beatrix made a practical contribution - some attractive dresses for the lady dancers.

In summer, the dancers performed on trim lawns, transferring in winter to a local hall. At Chapel Stile, in Great Langdale, dancing took place above a local store. One evening, dancers, including some from Sawrey, left the room to find it had been snowing heavily. In winter, the dancers gathered in the school at Far Sawrey, where Mrs Fyldes, known locally as Birdy Fyldes, played the piano. "We danced *Pick up Sticks, Bishop, Comical Fella, If all the World were Paper, Newcastle, Old Mole...*" Beatrix was to recall a night when she, Willie and some dancers travelled back to Sawrey in "frosty starlight." She also remembered the "mad barbaric music" played for a performance of the Kirkby Malzeard sword dance at Coniston. In 1929, when Beatrix and Willie attended a folk dancing festival at Underley Hall, near Kirkby Lonsdale, it inspired her to draw a picture of an imaginative *Dance of the Leaf Fairies.*

At Underley, in 1930, when the big annual festival gathering took place by invitation of Lord and Lady Henry Cavendish Bentinck, about 1,000 dancers took part and there was an equally large number of spectators. Clara Boyle, of Ambleside, was to recall that Willie danced his *Newcastle* and *Old Mole* with the best, reflecting credit on the Sawrey team. "Then came the great moment, when the three oldest men dancers of the Lake District - Mr Brady, the seventy-year-old little postmaster of Sedgwick, still an ardent rock-climber; Kenneth Spence of Sawrey House, and Mr Heelis, danced by themselves the old *Greensleeves* morris jig, which, in its buffoonery, demands an appreciable amount of agility, sense of rhythm and of fun. The three elderly men acquitted themselves with honour, in spite of their having had only one real practice together. Mrs Heelis was radiant with pride."

Ethel Byers was one of the Sawrey folk dance team driven to a dancing event by Willie Heelis. Four of the passengers sat in a "dicky" seat at the back of the car. It was a foggy night. Willie, who was not a good driver at the best of times, followed the tail lights of one or two vehicles and eventually came to a halt in a cul de sac. It was someone's drive. Willie was still greatly devoted to folk dancing when Clara Boyle tried to revive interest in the Ambleside district. "He was approaching the canonical age, and had become somewhat deaf, yet he came regularly to the weekly gatherings I organised at Sawrey and Hawkshead. He was always acompanied by his wife, who never danced a step and did not look as if she could, so stumpy and bent was she by that time. While Mr Heelis, like the other men, sported his white flannels and open-necked shirt, his wife sat in her rough, dark tweed skirt, pinned up behind with a large safety pin, with a tight-fitting bodice. She always looked out of place on such festival occasions - unless you observed her sweet smile and the loving eyes with which she followed every move of her Willie, lit up with the lamp of comradeship and devotion."

Beatrix joined Willie on some of his angling expeditions to Moss Eccles Tarn, half of which belonged to her. Tom Storey used to row the boat for him while Beatrix looked around or chattered now and again about things she could see up the intake. "She was fascinated by sheep and lambs and wanted to know who owned which stock of sheep." It was Tom, not Beatrix, who rowed their flat-bottomed boat. Whenever he heard anyone saying that Beatrix took up the oars, he would say: "Nowt o' t'sooart; she couldn't row that gurt big boat." Not that there was much rowing. "You just had to keep it moving." Beatrix had stocked the tarn with brown trout and, by gow, her husband could fish. "I've seen him throw a fly a long way and he used to catch a lot of fine trout. He'd give me some, but my family didn't care a big lot for them; they tasted a bit 'mossy'." On one warm June night in 1924, Beatrix and Willie, after being afloat on a windless, midgeless tarn, walked homewards at the especially late hour of 11 p.m.

When Sir William Hyde Parker, her cousin, and his wife Ulla, visited the Heelis's for a few days on their way to Scotland, they were surprised at how ordinary their cottage looked, and how small and dark was the dining-cum-living room. The pungent smell was later revealed to be that of sheepskins being cured in another room. The small kitchen was flagged, the flags being kept clean and shiny through being regularly washed by a mixture of milk and water. Cousin Beatie was recalled by Ulla as "a short, round little lady with a smiling rose face and small bright blue twinkling eyes." She was, of course, clad in tweed, of a brownish hue, the skirt almost touching the ground. She had a durable jersey. On her head was a straw hat, black in colour, with a piece of elastic extending from each side and passing under the chin of the wearer. Indoors, Beatrix doffed the hat and donned a white muslin mop cap.

Willie Heelis had a kindly face, a fresh complexion, grey hair and relaxed manner. Josephina Banner recalls meeting Willie, "a very good-looking man, a very charming country gentleman-lawyer. They were devoted to each other." A story began to circulate that she did not think much of him and spoke desparagingly of him. That didn't mean a thing, says Josephina, adding: "It was a term of endearment. It's like shepherds swearing at their dogs. The dogs would think they were unloved if they were not sworn at now and again!" The Banners were at Castle Cottage when it was close to supper-time at the back-end of the year. "Beatrix said: 'Wait and see Willie'. We waited quietly and she laid the table and put the silver candlesticks on it and lit the candles - and we felt we had been forgotten. She was looking forward to welcoming him home."

Josephina added: "It was romantic - one of those moments that is a poetic moment in life. When he came in, you could see by the way they looked at each other that it was a real love-match."

Children at Sawrey

MRS RICHARDS, the former Annie Black, was a girl at school when Beatrix came to live permanently at Sawrey. "I think most children feared her, and she never had any conversation with us. If anyone appeared unfriendly, they were regarded as strange. It was best to avoid her."

The Black family did not often see Beatrix, for they lived well out of the village, but one day Mr Black received a message. He should send Annie, his daughter, and her little brother, to Hill Top to receive a book. "We must be clean and tidy, making sure to take a linen bag in which to bring the book home. All the children of school age got the same invitation, and I can tell you there were threats and tears, for we did not want to go. Beatrix Potter received us and she was kind and pleasant. We were told to take care of the books. Mine was *The Tale of Two Bad Mice* and my brother's *The Tale of Peter Rabbit*."

If Beatrix scared the children, they did at least get amusement from the sight of the carriage and pair, with its attendant coachman and footman, wearing tall hats and cockades. They were father and son. There was never a smile nor a flick of an eye when they were on duty. This trim outfit belonged to Beatrix Potter's mother, who came to reside near the village. Anne Richards smiled as she remembered her father saying: "There's summat wrong wi't lot of 'em. They don't look quite reight to me."

When, following her marriage, Warnes tended to pester her about new books to meet the insatiable demand for her work, Beatrix was more happily occupied with farming matters. She had no interest in achieving popularity and, she confessed, did not care tuppence for modern children, who were pampered and spoilt with too many toys and books. Her unusual frostiness may have been induced by worries about the late arrival of her royalty cheques. There was trouble at Warnes, the publishers. The situation at a re-styled London publishing house soon improved.

Beatrix was not comfortable in the company of children because in her young days she was not accustomed to meeting those of her own age. She had a lonely childhood in a big London house. Her mother had not allowed her to invite children into the house for fear of transmitting germs - or being an undesirable influence. At Near Sawrey, in later life, if Beatrix was not popular with local children, she did at least have their respect. She could be sharp with them if they went near her sheep. She could be kind and occasionally organised parties.

Mrs Margaret Burns, of the Tower Bank Arms at Sawrey, said that Beatrix was good to local children - if they behaved themselves. "Lots of people thought her hard. I've never thought so. I think she was good." Her daughter, Willow, born and bred in Sawrey, confesses to being scared of Beatrix. If, during a ball game - which invaluably took place on the main road - the ball went over the wall into the Post Office meadow, it was ten-to-one that Mrs Heelis would be coming along the lane just as Willow was climbing the wall to get the ball. After rebuking the trespasser, she would go to Willow's father, at the inn, and complain of his youngest daughter's naughtiness.

Beatrix was able to converse more freely with teenagers, judging from the recollections of Willow, who as a teenager was able to share a conversation with her, and Winifride Bonney Bower, writing to me from Canada in 1986. "During some of my teenage years, from 1928 to 1930, I used to cycle on Saturday mornings from Coniston to Croft Head, High Wray, for my music lessons from Mrs Emily Keele. Many, many times while I was pushing my bicycle up the steep hills, I fell in with Mrs Heelis and walked along with her. She was walking between two of her sheep farms. Perhaps she routinely inspected these on Saturday mornings.

"She had the reputation of disliking children, but my experience was that she was consistently gracious and charming to me and a most pleasant companion on the road. I even recollect one of the jokes she told me. It concerned a Professor at Oxford who wrote in chalk on a notice board: 'Professor Black will meet his classes tonight at 7 p.m.' A student wag wiped out the 'c' in classes. Professor Black noticed the change from classes to lasses, so he wiped out the letter 'l'. Thus the third and final reading on the notice board was: 'Professor Black will meet his asses tonight at 7 p.m.'

"Mrs Heelis always wore on her walks the same heavy-looking, rather long, pepper and salt mixture tweed coat and skirt and boots. I really enjoyed our conversations and was always happy to catch up with her and walk along in her delightful company. Mrs Heelis told me that Coleridge had lodged in a farmhouse in the Lake District and that after he had left, the farmer's wife found some of Coleridge's manuscripts in a disused oven. I have often wondered if this story was true and, if so, what happened to those manuscripts."

One night there was a sing-song at the Tower Bank Arms, when Lakeland hunting songs were being rendered by the village folk to celebrate a John Peel anniversary. Beatrix Potter would not come into the building. But she paced up and down outside, listening to the music.

Tom Storey said: "Local children tended to be frightened of Mrs Heelis. If they were making a noise - which kiddies do - she would go out and tell them about it, till they got scared of her." Tom thought she was rather "funny" with children. "I had a little boy and girl when I came down to these parts in 1926. She thought the world of the boy, possibly because he was very keen on farming, though only four years old. She didn't like the girl." The lass asked him if she could play in the hayfield, and approval was given, though Tom added that she must play there by herself. She must not let anyone else come with her. "By gum, she hadn't been in long when Beatrix landed in t'field. Whether or not she heard kiddies playing, or she'd seen her, I don't know. She ordered her out. Then she went across with a frock skirt of her own for my wife to make her some decent clothes. She thought she should have been dressed like herself, not like any other child, but down to t'ground. She hadn't liked her playing in the field when the haytime men were there."

The Christmas party for the children of Sawrey is well remembered by Amanda Thistlethwaite. It was held at Castle Cottage on a Saturday afternoon, from 3 p.m. until 6 p.m. "She used to open up her sitting room. She had all the things taken to other parts of the house and we always started with tea, served in a big room upstairs, after which we'd come downstairs and dance. Mr Heelis played the pianola. He always started with a folk dance, *Roger de Coverley.* We children were aged from about five to ten. There'd be thirty of us. Mrs Heelis dressed herself up in her black satin and she was the life and soul of the party."

Christmas cake, jelly and other party food had been prepared by Mrs Rogerson. Beatrix took Amanda into a small room and showed her a book she had written. "You know what children are like. I was perhaps hoping she would give that book to me. She did give me it in the end. It was the only thing she ever gave me, except my wedding present - a cheque for £2. I should have kept that cheque, shouldn't I?" After telling me about the parties for children, Amanda observed: "As she got older, she got rather bitter against children. I feel it was because times had altered. Children were now more 'forward' and she couldn't abide that."

Edna Benson, reared at Troutbeck Park, remembers "a little old lady wearing a black shawl," adding that "we children were more interested in the chauffeur, Old Walter, who had a pocketful of sweets for us." Every year, Edna received a book from Beatrix. "She used to come to Troutbeck Park quite often and just before Christmas one year she said to my mam: "What have you bought Edna for Christmas?' Mam said: 'I've bought her a twin-set'. 'What colour?' 'Red'. 'Oh, Mrs Benson, you must take it back to the shop. If your little girl is out where there are some bullocks, they'll chase her'. My Mam had to take that twin-set back and she got me a blue one." Anthony Benson believes that she did good in many unpublicised ways. "In her time, many people were poor. The farthest thought in their heads would be to have owt much for dinner. . . Many a time, such as on a Sunday, Beatrix would bob 'em a joint o' meat."

Did Beatrix truly dislike children? One suspects that it was the modern child, "pampered and spoilt," she did not care to meet. Children who knew their places and were not cheeky were treated well. And, after all, The Tale of Benjamin Bunny, one of her best books, was dedicated thus:

FOR THE CHILDREN OF SAWREY
from
OLD MR BUNNY

Off to Troutbeck

TROUTBECK PARK, which she purchased in 1923, was her pet farm, according to Tom Storey. She visited the place regularly. Her chauffered car turned off the main road to follow an indifferent route up the bottom of the dale, the sides of which had a scattering of thorn trees. Tom, who worked for Beatrix for many years, was a lile chap, born in Barrow-in-Furness, who explained his wheeziness by saying that he was pigeon-chested, hence his move from town to the cleansing air of the Lake District. Naturally, he took up farming. Beatrix sought him out, took him on at Troutbeck, asked him to go to Sawrey to select two of Beatrix's lambs for Keswick Show, and then transferred him to Hill Top, where he might concentrate on rearing good show-sheep.

At Troutbeck Farm, said Tom, Beatrix would take a sandwich with her and go for a walk on the Tongue. She visited the fell in any sort of weather, and sometimes with a collie dog, with Nip or Fly. The Lakeland sheepdog, Artful Dodger of the hills, impressed her by its intelligence and obedience. Without it, life on the hill farms would be difficult, even impossible, for there would be no quick way of rounding up the sheep, for one of the seasonal jobs or when the snow-dogs were howling and the sheep must be driven into the dale.

Beatrix, visiting Troutbeck Tongue on almost every visit, seemed impervious to its soggy state, while describing it as uncanny, "a place of silences and whispering echoes. It is a mighty table-land between two streams. They rise together, north of the Tongue, in one maze of bogs and pools." The Tongue, lying between the becks, had an island status. There was always something of interest. One day, she crouched behind a boulder and and watched four of the native fell ponies going round and round in measured canter. She now had the answer to a puzzle, a

multitude of small unshod footprints, "much too small for horses' foot-
marks, much too round for deer or sheep." They had been fell ponies,
which were widely used to carry shepherds about the fells or as useful
shaft-animals in a lile cart.

Tom recalled that, on arriving at Troutbeck Farm, she would leave her
car in the farmyard and away she'd go through t'fold. "If I happened to
be away up t'fell, she'd go to Tongue End and wait for me coming back.

She carried a stick, not a crook, with her." Tom would eventually return
from leuking sheep, sit with her for a while and report whatever had happened. "It wasn't often she could be persuaded to come into t'farm kitchen for a drink o' tea. She just had her sandwiches, which were wrapped in a piece of paper. She ate 'em outside."

Troutbeck Park, one of Lakeland's largest sheep farms, is at the
dalehead, flanked by the lean ridges of fells which form the skirts of
mighty High Street. The farm, now over two and a-half thousand acres,
lies behind a ring fence. In the valley are thirty acres of meadowland.

As hill farms go, Troutbeck Park is a good one. The crags might be draped with snow and ice for months on end. The farm buildings, painted white in the local tradition, show up well against the summer greens and are Lilliputian in scale when viewed from a lay bye on the road from Windermere to Kirkstone. Then the observer might actually look down on a buzzard which is circling and mewing.

Behind the buildings rises The Tongue (from an Old Norse word meaning "a ridge between two valleys that join"). It is a soggy place. Ravens nesting on the crags call with gruff voices and then flick on to their backs during flight, as though for the sheer joy of living. In accordance with the wishes of Beatrix, a stock of Herdwick sheep is maintained alongside the now customary Swaledale sheep. The Herdwicks might be found grazing on High Street. "When you come to look at the Herdwicks on the real Herdwick fells in the west - around Eskdale and Wasdale - you'll find that they are only half the size of those kept at Troutbeck Park. Here the 'going' is better. . . We always say in snowtime that it's a pity the walkers don't take notice of the hill sheep. They known the safest, most sheltered places."

When the Tyson family moved to Troutbeck Farm, they had not known Beatrix but heard many tales about her. The fireplace in the living room was made by Mr Storey, a local builder, under Beatrix's supervision, using pieces from the old metal fireplace, which had liberal applications of black-lead, and local stone, with sandstone pillars. On the sandstone slab above the fireplace was carved an inscription, "A honest heart and tarry woo'," which was taken from an old Cumbrian song about tarry wool. Mr Storey's son, Charles, who was then a small boy, recalled that Beatrix stood over his father, telling him where each stone should be placed.

It was said that the only person she was afraid of was her chauffeur. When he was ready to leave the farm for the return to Sawrey, he would mention it to her. Once, she did not go out immediately. So he left her.

Beatrix was never late again. Beatrix was said to surreptitiously feed the mice in the farm kitchen. "When we came here, there were lots of mice. You might be baking in the kitchen and they would run out of their holes and appear round the table. We tried catching them with plastic bowls. It was hopeless. Fortunately, we do not have any mice now." At dusk, in winter, it is not unusual for a few red deer to graze the low ground. Badgers shuffle about looking for food. The scattering of trees on the steep fellside attract nesting buzzards, which mew as they circle in the updraught.

It was at Troutbeck Park that I was shown a room especially associated with her. It was her study, when she wanted it, which was not often, for she preferred on her visits to the Park to be out of doors, watching the seasonal tasks with sheep - lambing, dipping, clipping, spaining - or wandering up on to the Tongue, here to sit and await the return of her shepherd, seeking up to date news about the sheep. The room contained furniture, pottery, also pictures she had drawn. I saw a decorative writing desk and a writing box, the top inlaid with mother-of-pearl. A chest of drawers and a cabinet were the major items. The firetongs and poker remained at the fireplace beside which Beatrix would have sat. A picture, featuring an animal, and said to have been a favourite of Willie Heelis, hung in this room. In the bottom of a wall cupboard was a pile of her notes, scribbles, and drawings of small animals. Over the years, the furniture became green mouldy and the farmer, if he ever went into the room, had to make his way through cobwebs to find anything. At the time of my visit, a cotton carpet and small woollen rug which belonged to Beatrix had been preserved by being placed under the carpet currently in use.

In the 1920s, Beatrix recruited Tom Storey, who had worked for Noble Gregg, of Troutbeck, for a dozen happy years and was not thinking of moving on. Beatrix sought him out, arriving unannounced at the Gregg farm, Town End, just as Tom was completing the hand-milking of a dozen Shorthorn cows. He had never even "heard tell on" her before that day. It was, as Tom recalled to me, 6 p.m. on an October Saturday in 1926 when Beatrix, "a little woman, and bonnie-looking," asked him his name and was told it. "She said: 'Well, I'm Mrs Heelis. I hear you're leaving Mr Gregg's farm'. I said: 'Yes'. She said: 'Will you come and work for me?' I said: 'Yes, I don't mind - if the money's right'. She asked: 'How old are you?' I said: 'I'm thirty'. She said: 'Oh - I'm sixty'. Just like that.

"She asked me how much I was getting as a wage. She was quite straight about it. I told her. 'Well', she said, 'if you work for me I'll double it'. I said it was all right. She asked me when I could start. I said I would start on Monday. I'd nowhere else to go and I was married then." Tom paused and added: "That's how it happened. I went to Troutbeck Park on the following Monday . . ."

I asked Tom for more background information about the visit to Town End of the celebrated Beatrix. Noble Gregg was known as a speedy milker, "and I wasn't bad miself." It took just five minutes to milk a cow. "We reckoned that one man could milk a dozen cows, if they were good to do, in an hour." On that November evening, in the shippon at Town End, a dozen Shorthorns were quietly dining on hay. "At five o'clock we cleaned them out; made their tubs; milked them, then 'fothered' them for the night."

What had prompted Beatrix to seek out Tom at Troutbeck? "I didn't find out till quite a long time after. Tommy Atkinson and his brother lived at the next farm to Hill Top. They had tried showing Herdwick sheep. They gave over because they couldn't make anything of it. Mrs Heelis had bought one or two of these sheep off them; she didn't want them to be sold and taken out of the district. News spread that I was leaving Town End. Mrs Heelis, who was wanting a man to look after her sheep, went round the district 'getting my character'. I heard that a while after! She went to the old farmers in the district who knew me." Her journey from Sawrey to Town End was in a brand-new, bull-nosed Morris Cowley, driven by Tommy Christie, of Colthouse, who was forester on the estate but "doubled up" as chauffeur.

In 1926, Tom Storey was married with two young children. He and his family lived at a cottage in the village. He was looking forward to living at Troutbeck Park, but before he had an opportunity of moving in, Beatrix asked him to take over at Hill Top, Sawrey. "She wanted to show Herdwick sheep. Why she couldn't show them from Troutbeck Park, I don't know, because there were about a thousand Herdwick ewes there." She had no sheep but Herdwicks and called other breeds "mongrels." When Tom said he would prefer to go to Troutbeck Park, she offered to augment his wage if he would manage the Sawrey farm instead. "I said: 'All right. If the wife's willing, then I'm willing to move to Sawrey'. That's how we landed. . . ."

Beatrix, having bought Troutbeck Park, and believing that Englishmen were no good among sheep, employed a Scotsman at the farm. "Her brother farmed in Scotland, you see. She got to know all about the Scottish ways, which were different from those we followed down here. She wanted the Scottish routine at Troutbeck Park, but folk laughed at her. And she learnt her lesson." Tom was at Troutbeck Park for twelve months, moving to Hill Top on June 15, 1927. At Troutbeck Park, he put rams on to a thousand breeding ewes and lambed them the following spring.

"It had been 'tipping time' when I went, being November. I marked 992 lambs out. You marked as many as you thought fit, and you forgot two or three that were left to lamb, because foxes would go with them." The mark for Troutbeck Park was red on the hook (where the thigh bone sticks up). "They hadn't had very good luck with lambing at Troutbeck Park because it was a devil of a farm for sheep fluke. There'd been no cure for it in those days. When I went to Troutbeck Park, the cure came from a veterinary firm at Newcastle. We got it in the form of capsules. By jove, we used it that back end, and it was a life-saver."

Anthony Benson first worked at Troutbeck Farm as a lad fresh from school. The farm was then owned by Mrs Leah. After a year, he moved away. He had a variety of jobs. When he was working for Isaac Fleming, he heard from Mr Heelis, who was Isaac's solicitor, that a shepherd was needed at Troutbeck Park. "I know a bit aboot that spot," said Anthony. Mr Heelis asked: "Would it be any good sending Mrs Heelis up to see you about it?" Anthony replied: "Aye. There's no harm." In due course, Beatrix arrived. Anthony inquired how much wage he would receive. He had been earning 25s. "Mrs Heelis offered me £4.10s straight off. She built us a cottage. She kept us in coal. She fed the dogs. (I always kept five or six dogs). With all the extras, that wage was as good as £6."

Anthony's wife, Sarah, was a "townie" from Workington. Mrs Heelis got on well with her. "One day, she asked me if I had a bank book. I said: 'I don't know what sort of a thing that is'. She told me about it and said that if I started a bank account, for every £1 put in she'd add £1. It went on for fifteen years." Anthony showed her the bank book when she came to pay him every fortnight. She saw to it that whatever he had put in the account was doubled.

They had their differences, of course. Beatrix and Anthony differed in their assessment of how a particular farm job should be done. "Watter used to run down one side of a fence. She wanted t'watter to come underneath that fence. She took me to it and showed me what had to be done. I said: 'That's wrong, Mrs Heelis'. She said: 'Who's paying for the job, Benson?' I said: 'It's still all wrong'. Said Beatrix: 'Well, do it your own way'. And she stomped off."

Beatrix was most happy walking with the springy turf underfoot and the mountain breeze in her face. "She was a lish body," recalls Anthony. "She would walk around the fields where there was a lot of sheep. Or she'd set off on a hill track." She found sheep clipping time, with its noise and bustle, most exhilarating. "We clipped between two thousand

and three thousand sheep - all Herdwicks. It took about seven hours simply to 'gather'. The sheep went as far as High Street and round by Caud'l. Before her day, there had been a boon clip, with neighbours helping. It was always on the last Tuesday in June."

Some local people sighed for the lost glories of the "boon clip." A meal had been served in the barn. "There were trestle tables. The main course was beef, new tatties and Yorkshire pudding." At night, when work was done, more refreshments were served and the day ended with dancing. "Under Mrs Heelis, we just clipped away by ourselves. I've seen us sit down of a morning at seven o'clock and clip, then git up and have our dinners, and back and sit down again, and clip till six o' clock. It went on maybe for a fortnight or three weeks. There were always four of us clipping. I was the shepherd, so many a day I didn't get sat down. I was away fetchin' some more sheep in. We fed well, but there was no 'do' afterwards."

At Troutbeck Park, Galloway cattle were reared for beef. "We had only one milk cow, for household use. If that cow ran dry, they took it down to Hill Top and fetched another. We'd always plenty o' milk." The Galloways were of good quality, from stock bought at Newcastleton, on the Borders. "I'd nowt to do with the cows," said Anthony. "My job was sheep. I never went wi' them when they were buying or selling cows. They used to take calves from Troutbeck to Newcastleton by motor wagon, and stay overnight. Mrs Heelis would go to t'bull sale."

After a serious illness in the late 1930s, her recuperation was assisted by visits to her beloved Troutbeck Park, where she watched the Herdwick sheep being clipped and saw her fine beef cattle. There were thirty cows, with calves at foot, and a white bull. She also attended Keswick Tup Fair. "She wore the same old costume, day in and day out. It was a thick tweed and reet doon to her ankles." Anthony never saw her judging sheep. "I've seen her looking at 'em. She didn't know a gurt lot about sheep. She was a body who took a lot o' notice of such as Old

Isaac Thompson, Ned Nelson and all them old flockmasters."

Anthony was one of those indomitable men who, in October, drove young sheep long distances from fell farms such as Troutbeck Park to winter grazings on lower land - an area that was overswept by mild breezes from the sea. "We used to take sheep, mainly shearlings, to Home Fell at Coniston and Tarn Hows. The hoggs (last year's lambs) went on to Birker Moor. We set off from Troutbeck Park as soon as it

came daylight and took maybe six hundred sheep altogether, in two trips. Two of us with two or three dogs drove sheep down to Lowwood and on to Waterhead, then ower Rathay Brigg, up to Skelwith Brigg and over top of Oxen Gill to Coniston. They just had a few sheep at Sawrey and Birker Moor was the farthest area we went. I've put some queer days in there."

In April, the Birker Moor sheep were walked to Tilberthwaite, where "we'd stop aw neet. Lile Tommy Stoddart was at Tilberthwaite then and he used to put us up overneet and help us next morning to come through by t'quarries to top of Oxen Fell. . .If you were on t'road wi' t'sheep, Mrs Heelis passed you three or four times to see that all was going well. If there was a lame dog, she'd pick it up, take it home and fetch you another dog. Mind you, if you were lame, she wouldn't. She watched the droving operation from her car, which was driven by Walter Stevens, a grand auld fella."

At lambing time, Joe Moscrop, a special "doctor" was accommodated at Troutbeck Park. He was from Scotland. "Mrs Heelis thought the world o' that man. He came every year I was there to look after the waifs and strays." Joe was a good sheep doctor. "He had a drop o' gin in a bottle, and he used to put two or three drops on to a lamb's tongue to warm it up. I've seen us working at dark o' neet, wi' just an old lamp. (We'd no electricity then)." Joe, an elderly man, was "a wiry old customer." His dog, Jess, was first-rate. Anthony tried to buy it off him. Several times he asked and several times he was refused. "It got to five pund, which was a big price then. I said: 'I'll gie thee five pun, Joe, for that dog. Just leave her. If she settles down it'll be OK. If she doesn't, she'll be here next time you come back.' I wanted it because it had a gey lot o' eye, and it was just the job for working on a felltop."

Anthony relates that Joe would go into the field with Jess and say: 'Catch me this, Jessie, please'. He always said please when addressing the dog. It used to make the other men laugh. The dog would enter the field and grab the desired sheep by the cheek, though it wouldn't mark it.

Beatrix had an old dog called Bob. "It was a lile bow-legged thing, though he'd been a good dog in his time. When I first went to Troutbeck Park, Mrs Heelis had four or five dogs of her own. I used to think that Bob was useless. But you had to take it with you." One day, Anthony and Bob reached an area on the fell where there was a sheep trod. "Bob wouldn't gang any further. It went along that trod and was never seen again . . . We wasted many a day looking for it. Mrs Heelis came up every day to help." Six or seven old dogs that had been pensioned off had a special kennel which she inspected whenever she visited Troutbeck Park. "The kennel had to be cleaned out properly."

When Anthony killed a badger, he thought he had done a good thing. Mrs Heelis got to know about it and asked for an explanation. "I said: 'Well a badger worries lambs and things like that'. She said: 'Oh, no it doesn't'. I nearly got my notice over the badger. She was reet upset." Beatrix disliked foxhunting, and she would not have the hunt on her land. She did agree to "summer" a hound for the local pack. Anthony said: "If there was a hunt not so far from Troutbeck Park in winter, I was missing."

Down on the Farm

FOLLOWING her marriage, Beatrix and Willie settled down to a quiet but busy life. She preferred to be known as Mrs Heelis. Her energies were directed towards farming and acquiring property. John Cannon and his wife occupied Hill Top, and the farmhouse had been enlarged so she had separate accommodation for herself at one end. The Cannons lived at the other. John was designated cowman, foreman and shepherd (when she first bought the farm, the livestock included sixteen Herdwick sheep). His wife was dairy woman and farm-housekeeper. Willie Cannon did the ploughing. Her old shepherd, Joseph Moscrop, helped with the lambing. Beatrix's favourite collie, Kep, was photographed with its proud owner.

On the farm were cattle, sheep and pigs. Many of the pigs were bought from Sally Scales, of Stott Farm, Graythwaite, west of Windermere. A pet pig, known as Sally, followed her round the village and responded whenever Beatrix called her name. There were hens and ducks. One duck had a hatch so wild they could not be caught, so Willie shot the drake. Some of her turkeys were killed by the pekes. She had a fondness for fell ponies, the old Lakeland breed, and was anxious when Lakeland breeders were tempted to use Clydesdale crosses.

Came the 1914-18 war, with its bureaucratic intrusion. Beatrix, concerned that the Army might demand the farm horses, said that "at a pinch we can use cattle." Beatrix did most of the cooking, attended to the poultry, the orchard and the garden. She assisted at haytime. Those were the days, as Josephina Banner recalled for me, "when we did proper haymaking and made hay-cocks and pikes." When Beatrix had time she might "single" the turnips. In 1916, Eleanor Choyce (known to her friends as Louie) came to help with the farming. She and her brother were given quarters at Hill Top. They were cautioned not to be rough with her old and valuable furniture. There was little time left for writing and illustrating books.

With the war over, Miss Choyce left in 1922. Beatrix kept in touch with her through letters and in the autumn of that year she described her life in farming. It had been a grim season, with wind gusting to gale force and rain sweeping in from the west. With the sea on three sides, and with high fells to create clouds, Lakeland had depressing spells of what Beatrix called "sea fog". The dalesfolk knew it as a "fret". Loads of corn or hay were snatched to safety during brief sunny periods. Hard work did pay off and little of the crop was spoiled but it was less than required and some cattle had to be sold off. The poultry had thrived. Fruit was plentiful but the apples, being small and unripe, blown from the branches of the trees, would have to be converted into apple and blackberry jelly.

When Tom Storey came into her life, first at Troutbeck Park, then from 1927 at Hill Top, he had a wife and two children. Tom succeeded

William Mackereth, who having worked for her for eleven years had retired in 1926 to spend his twilit years at Maryport. Tom Storey's goods were transferred to Sawrey using a motor lorry. Tom was both a cattle and a sheep man. At Hill Top, he found the land was hard and sound. "It couldn't bide too much dry weather, though." The garden was almost a wilderness. Despite her creation of Peter Rabbit, and the fact that she was breeding rabbits, Beatrix did not object to the men trapping bunnies in the wild. She sent a brace of rabbits to Mrs Cannon just before Christmas.

When Tom began to restore some of the natural balance, he found that a vast number of rabbits retarded the grass growth. Hardly any farm stock could be kept. Rabbits also abounded on Beatrix's seventy acres of land beyond Esthwaite Water. Tom told me: "Jack Hird snared these rabbits in October. In one month he caught nine hundred. A wood near Hill Top belonged to the next estate. It was full of rabbits. They grazed on Mrs Heelis's land, an area known as The Heights. Willie Heelis and Captain Duke went out with a net, rigged it up near the wood, left the net furled until the rabbits had passed, then slipped the netting down in the hope of catching rabbits as they sped for cover." It was a good idea which did not work too well in practice. "Those rabbits were cute, you know."

Tom Storey and the farm man toiled on a farm which had scarcely any labour-saving implements or machines. "Mrs Heelis didn't try to keep up with the times. Everyone had haytime implements, except us. We did at least have a mowing machine." The cattle were Shorthorn, hand-milked, though Beatrix had invested in a separator to replace the churn for separating the cream from the milk, for the production of butter or milk. What remained - the so-called "blue" milk - was fed to the young stock. No one grieved at the passing of churning, especially when they thought of how slow was the process in hot weather. One of Tom's morning tasks was to pour some milk into a can and take it to Castle Cottage for domestic use. It was a ritual which pleased Beatrix, who would meet him at the door, eager not only to have a supply of milk but to learn about the latest happenings at Hill Top.

Tom Storey used to "butch" at Hill Top. Beatrix had a licensed slaughter-house and at t'back-end she arranged for lambs to be "butched" and the meat to be taken round the village. Lamb was sold at about 6d a pound. Tom was known for his ability to slaughter pigs and went round the district attending to the pigs of others. Beatrix did not care much for pig-keeping, having had a "disappointment" some years before, when a litter did not thrive.

Josephina Banner recalls that she first met Beatrix Potter through farming. She and her husband Delmar were very closely connected with the folk of Eskdale, she having carved Old Benny Armstrong's tombstone, which is on his grave in the yard of St Catherine's church, Eskdale. The coffin had been borne there on a horse-drawn cart, with a great throng of dalesfolk to pay their last respects.

"I was helping with the Eskdale Show, washing up at the Woolpack or serving dinners to the farmers in the big barn, wearing boiler suit and clogs, my natural working dress as a sculptor, when I was introduced to Beatrix by Cyril Bulman who, with his wife Sally, had come to help their relations at the Woolpack. Beatrix had travelled to the show in an antiquated, strange-looking car, very much like a taxi. And it was driven by an ancient chauffeur, whose face was so lined, I said to her once: 'Was your chauffeur a lizard?' meaning the type of lizard in Cinderella. She said, slowly: 'Maybe'."

Beatrix was in her best tweedy suit, coat and skirt, "a sort of browny-green," which included "a beautiful fluffy felt hat with elastic under the chin to keep it on. Of course, there were clogs on her feet. She carried an umbrella which had belonged to Mr Warne, the man whom she was engaged to and who died. Unhappily, too, while haymaking at Sawrey she had lost the ring he gave her." Beatrix loved to share in haymaking, though such frolics were forbidden by her doctor. One year, she tossed hay. She recounted to Josephina: "My belt-support slipped off, and down I fell." She told this with a twinkle in her eyes. "I felt such a fool; they had to carry me in."

Shortly before Cyril introduced the Banners to Beatrix, she had been judging the rams and ewes and had subsequently wandered around, looking at stock in the pens. "You could see by the manner of the farmers that they thought the world of her. A great big tall farmer who had had too much to drink, was too friendly. He came along, walking like a heron, on very long legs, and he slapped her on the back. The blow was so hard it nearly toppled her over. She staggered. He said: 'I knew John Peel. At least my father knew him. And there were times when he was so drunk they had to put him on his horse'. Beatrix, without looking at him - she went on looking at a ram - said: 'I never thought owt o' John Peel'. It was a brave thing to say in front of those farmers."

Beatrix, having been introduced to the Banners, was impressed when she saw that Josephina was wearing clogs. "We got on. We were both very straight-forward people." Beatrix later discovered her new friends were artists. "She was very sensitive and knew a great deal about me I did not need to tell her. When someone asked me what she was like, I said 'It's like being a person who'd been eating white bread all his or her life and suddenly come across a brown loaf'."

Beatrix Potter and the Lake District became one. Josephina and Delmar were staying at the Woolpack, in Eskdale, when they met a Professor from Durham. "He was to do with the farming. He told us he had recently sent out a questionaire about sheep to some of the leading farmers in our district. The most interesting reply had come from a farmer called Heelis." The professor wrote to him and mentioned he would be in the Sawrey district one day and would it be possible to have a meeting? "I got a nice letter back saying: 'Yes, do'. So I made the appointment and went to Castle Cottage, Sawrey, where the door was opened by a tiny, old, traditionally-dressed maid, in stiff black and white, like a Victorian doll.

"I went upstairs to a bedroom at the top of the stairs which was mostly taken up by a huge double bed. And in the middle of it a tiny old lady, looking very pretty, in her big jacket and hair tied up with a black velvet bow. This was Farmer Heelis. I had tea with her. It was brought up on

a tray. We talked about sheep complaints." The professor had been enchanted by her unique and delightful personality and by her unpretentious realism. Beatrix told Josephine that when she was in that bed, she used to look through the window and there was just one cabbage left in the garden. It looked terrible. "I kept on saying: 'Pull up that cabbage'. And nobody did it. One day, when nobody was looking, I put on two pairs of knickers and my husband's raincoat and I went out and tugged it up." Oh, added Josephine - she was delightful.

Beatrix's purchase of the Monk Coniston estate brought remote little

Tilberthwaite into her ownership. In the early 1930s, her farm manager was Tommy Stoddart, a tiny, round fellow who was very cheerful. He moved into the main farm with his wife Florrie, also two sons and a daughter. Meanwhile, at Sawrey, Hill Top continued to be run on traditional lines. Then, wonder of wonders, during the 1939-45 war a tractor appeared. A Hawkshead woman who worked at The Glen, noticed that after the tractor had been round the hayfield, Beatrix would scuffle about near the hedge all round the field, pulling bits of hay into the open. When the outbreak of war brought staff shortages, Miss Choyce returned to help out. Beatrix, who liked to be mobile, lamented petrol rationing. During a flu epidemic, she wrote to a friend: "Keep Smiling!" Many letters were written and signed H B Heelis, which would mean nothing to a person conditioned by looking at her books to think of her as Beatrix Potter.

During the war, wool prices improved wonderfully. Beatrix bought Galloway bulls from a breeder in the Carlisle area. She spent £20 on a portable wooden silo and declared that this new-fangled silage was "almost better than cake." The Ministry of Agriculture insisted on her growing potatoes at Troutbeck Park. Old Joseph Moscrop helped with the lambing and minor tasks at clipping-time. Shortly before she died, with the war at its most intense, Beatrix took up paper and pencil and wrote a letter to Joe who, despite her great respect for Tom Storey, remained her favourite among those who tended the sheep.

In Love with Herdwicks

BEATRIX took a close interest in farming. If she kept interfering when the men were trying to work at Hill Top, Tom Storey would quietly remark: "I wish she'd get oot o' t'spot." When it came to sheep, and Beatrix was attending a Keswick Show or the autumn sales at Ambleside, she showed deference to others. Tom was breeding the sort of Herdwick sheep which won awards. Beatrix loved the atmosphere of the shows and the company of the old fellside farmers who formed little groups. She received any prize cards rapturously.

The Herdwicks which were her pride and joy were most at home on the high fells, such as those round Troutbeck Park. The Sawrey countryside was really too soft for them. Wiry and goat-like, this breeed has deep round bodies and rough white faces - a race influenced perhaps less than any other by the introduction of outside blood, though considerable improvements had been made by selective breeding early last century. Thick-boned, sweet-fleshed, the Herdwick is thatched by a fleece that is more like hair than wool, fit only in man's world for carpets and coarse tweeds, but perfectly suited to the climate and conditions of England's highest mountains.

In her frequent visits to Troutbeck Park, and her walks on the Tongue, she saw Herdwicks which, in her day, if not today, did not take readily to special rations like hay. She rejoiced in that pride. If they were pampered, the vital heaf-going instinct, by which they keep to specific areas of a fell, might be disturbed. The Herdwick is a character. I can imagine that as Beatrix walked on a sheep-speckled fellside, she would be amused when, straying on to a part of the fell being used by a particular ewe, she would hear a disdainful sneeze. The Herdwick is as much a stay-at-home as an old fellside farmer and knows its place on a fell for that was where it took in its mother's milk.

Beatrix was fond of lambing time, when a Herdwick ewe which had carried its lamb for twenty of the grimmest weeks in the year parted with the infant, which initially was black but would go greyer with age. The nuptials had been in November, or even December. No one expected the Lakeland weather to improve until the birthtime in April or May, for spring is slow in coming to the fells and the daleheads. As the snow and ice melted from the high grazings, the Herdwicks reached for the newly-exposed vegetation, keeping the grassy areas of the fells as fine and close-cut as a bowling green. Then came the time for ewes to be quartered in the dalehead fields, where the shepherd could keep an eye on them and be handy when the lambs appeared.

Beatrix became so much attached to some Herdwicks that they had names. One of them was Water Lily, who eventually, having reached the geriatric stage of life, and with over a dozen lambs to her credit, was retired from the show ring because, as Beatrix wrote to Miss Choyce in 1934, "I could see she was embarrassing to the judges!" Like some old dalehead farmer, to whom thriftiness was next to godliness, Beatrix was keen, when buying something like sheep dip, to have a discount for cash. And when she bought sheep, she demanded "a bit of luck," as was customary, a coin passed from the buyer to the seller ensuring good luck. She lived through a time when a halfbred lamb was valued at about £1 but when the top price for Beatrix's lambs was appreciably more at 26s. Herdwick wool, which on the fell-going sheep turned a hundred inches of rain a year, was of poor quality commercially. "The price sticks at fourpence," she noted in a letter to a friend.

John Fishwick, an auctioneer's clerk who later became an auctioneer, recalls that Beatrix could be testy when someone, usually a small boy, interfered with her beloved Herdwicks when they were penned at a show and had nowhere to run. When John was fifteen years old he attended the autumnal sheep sales at Ambleside. Beatrix had surplus sheep moved from Troutbeck Park to Rawthey Holme, at Ambleside, where the pens were placed on land between the sewage works and the council office.

As a clerk, John toured the pens with pencil and notepad, recording the number of sheep each person had on sale that day. "As soon as Mrs Heelis had booked in her stock, she would say to me: 'You be off, young laddie. Go and see Mr So-and-so; he wants to give you the information about his sheep'. A few children stayed off school to go to the sheep sale. If they looked at the pens where her sheep were, she would chase them away, telling them: 'Keep off. Keep off. Go away'!" Beatrix was not then widely known for her writings. She is recalled as a stocky woman who wore coarsely woven clothes, with a pork-pie type hat and with clogs on her feet. She was usually in the company of her shepherds - of Tom Storey and George Walker, the last named being at Troutbeck Park.

Beatrix's fascination with the distinctive sheep breed of the Lake District began as long ago as 1903. She sketched the distinctive sheep marks of the area around Fawe Park, Keswick, where she was on holiday with her family. She wrote movingly of the demise at Hill Top of an outstanding Herdwick ram, "a grand old champion of the fells. . ." This was Josiah Cockbain's splendid animal, Saddleback Wedgewood, which was "the perfect type of hard, big-boned Herdwick tup, with strong clean legs, springy fetlocks, broad scope, fine horns, a grand jacket and mane. He had strength without coarseness. A noble animal."

When her interest in the Herdwick breed developed into a desire to own some, she consulted Joseph Gregg, who sold her the first sheep of this breed she owned. Joe, born in Great Langdale in 1883, had a break from farming during the 1914-18 war, being wounded during Army service in France. Back in Lakeland, he resumed farming, eventually becoming tenant at Town End, Troutbeck. Joe's son, Vic, told me: "My father and his brother, Noble Gregg, had a lot of surplus sheep to be sold at Ambleside. I still have the prices that they made that day. Lambs were being sold for 3s.6d to 5s.6d." Vic, who attended Lakeland sheep sales and shows with his father, recalls Beatrix as a quaint old lady wearing dark clothes. "She knew my father and she'd give me a copper or two."

The Gregg family moved to Taw House, at the head of Eskdale, and Beatrix was in part concerned with their return from Eskdale to Great Langdale in 1935. Willie Heelis, her husband, had to deal with Millbeck, in Langdale, when it was bought by Professor Trevelyan. Beatrix, hearing it was available to let, and remembering the kindnesses shown to her by Joe Gregg when she bought Troutbeck Park, instructed her chauffeur to drive her to Taw House. Vic recalls: "We were carting bracken for bedding. To see a car coming into the yard of Taw House was something of a rarity. We were having tea. Mrs Heelis came to the door and said: 'Joe - I want a word with you'. They went through into the sitting room, where she was offered the customary cup of tea and piece of cake.

"That night, father said: 'I'll not be here when you get up in the morning. You'll have to milk the cows and look after yourself. I'm going to Kendal'. He did not say what for. When he got back that night, he told us we would be moving to Millbeck in the spring. Mrs Heelis had made it possible by recommending him for the tenancy." Says Vic: "She was serious about the Herdwick sheep. If there was a sheep show, she'd be there. She wouldn't miss anything."

Tom Storey's happiest memories of Beatrix was from the time when she began to show off her best Herdwick sheep at the Lakeland shows. Indeed, he had not been long at Troutbeck Park when she asked him to go to Sawrey and pick out two Herdwick lambs to be exhibited at Keswick. Each won a first prize at the show, to the delight of Beatrix, who told her shepherd that these were the first prizes she had ever won. Henceforth, no other breed had to be kept on her farms, though on a "fell spot" like Troutbeck Park, it was not always easy to keep the flock pure. Stray tups came in from other places.

Tom went with her to many of the fell shows, including Ennerdale, Loweswater, Gosforth and Eshd'l (Eskdale). "If she lost, she didn't grumble. In her time, she won all the big prizes." Her favourite outfit was made of Herdwick tweed. "Once she gave me three fleeces from our show ewes and I had a suit made up from the wool. That suit was cut in the late 'thirties'. It's rough tweed - but it still [1980s] wears well."

Beatrix was saddened at the death of Canon H D Rawnsley, who had founded the Herdwick Sheepbreeders' Association. He wrote romantically about the Herdwick, as the following passage indicates: "The shepherd knows that a lamb suckled on its native 'heaf' or pasturage will never forget it, and though it be taken by force from the hills, if it have only been mothered there for fourteen days, it will drink in such a homing instinct with its mother's milk, as will guide it back over hill and dale to the pasturage of its infancy...Very interesting it is to watch the shepherds take them to the fell. They do not open a gate and let them scatter where they will, rather...they take them to the furthest part of the pasture they are to range, furthest that is from the farm in the valley, and there leave them. Instinctively the flock knows its utmost limit and will begin to feed backwards towards the dale."

Anthony Benson told me that on the showfield all the old flockmasters liked to talk to Mrs Heelis. Among the wise old men of the hill farms was Herdwick Billy, who started off in Borrowdale and was eventually running sheep on Binsey, near Bassenthwaite Lake. He called his house Herdwick Croft and incorporated an impression of a Herdwick sheep in stained glass. Isaac Thompson, who used to be at West End, Wythburn, and Edward (Ned) Nelson o' Gatesgarth, were two other "auld fellas" with lots to say about Lakeland's own little breed of sheep. Beatrix was "yan o' those who'd tak a fancy to a particular sheep, when there were mebbe plenty better 'uns."

The old-timers had minds packed with the lore of sheep. Anthony said: "At places like Keswick, you used to hire a tup. It would cost £1, £2 or £3. If it were a good 'un, mebbe more. You used that tup and had to winter it till May, when you took it to the spring show and returned it to its owner, paying him for being able to use it." Herdwick tups on show day were splendid animals. "They were weshed up an' ivverything." They wore "show red," their fleeces having been smeared with red rudd. In due course, the old hiring custom began to give way to outright sales. There was a keen demand for the best tups. "If Mrs Heelis wanted one, she would have it. She once paid nearly £200 for a tup, and £200 was a lot of money in those days."

Beatrix was driven to the sheep shows by her husband, the un-complaining Willie Heelis, in his little Ford car. Meanwhile, Tom Storey, her manager, and his helpers had been out of their beds at 5 a.m. "I milked twelve cows then. The show sheep were kept in a handy pasture and we had a lile lorry to transport 'em. Tommy Christopherson drove the lorry. We took a shearling and a hogg, two tups, a two-shear tup, two ewes, a couple of two-shears, four twinters and two lambs. Mrs Heelis never saw the sheep till the time I brought them into the far-myard, just before a show, and put the 'show red' on 'em. You had to be particular about this. You could get too much 'red' on and then it'd spoil the look of 'em. I used to wash their faces and their legs with soap and water. I did it again when I'd got them in the pen at the show ground." Tom's sheep were ready for showing at 10 a.m. "Then Mrs Heelis would turn up, in a car, and make over towards them."

Tom added: "Folk thought yon sheep got fed, but they didn't. I proved that with Jimmy from Knott Houses at Grasmere. He came down one Sunday with Teddy Tyson, who used to show a lot. We'd looked at t'show sheep, which were down t'bottom meadow. Jimmy said: 'I don't see any troughs in that field'. I said: 'No, thou wean't. Them sheep don't get any feed i'summer. Nobbut i' winter'. 'Oh', I said, 'I always feed my show sheep through summer'. He said: 'I don't. They last longer if they don't get too much feed'." The first trophy to be won for her was award-ed to one of her shearlings at Hawkshead in 1928; two years later, her sheep claimed any number of major prizes at the shows, and when she won the cup marked Ennerdale, Loweswater, Eskdale, 1930, "for cham-pion female", she retained the original trophy and had a copy made for Tom, who was also allowed to retain teapots and tankards.

Tom and others were wrily amused at a show when Beatrix didn't "ken" her own sheep. At Keswick, where she was photographed with Lady Leconfield, she later talked her way to the sheep pens. "All the old sheep farmers knew her. She'd talk for a week to a real old sheep farmer. I was standing there talking to two men; we were leaning on the pens and straight across were our sheep. She walked down the side of the pens with old Mr Mackereth, who was a hind before I came to Hill Top. As it happened, I was showing one sheep that she should have known. It was one of t'elder sheep, a ewe. I saw them walking near the pens, then stop suddenly. She talked about sheep. Then she whipped round and said: 'Which is such-and-such ewe, Storey, among these?' I said: 'Them aren't yours. Yours are in t'next pen'. Was her face red! I don't think she liked it but she daren't say anything. I was only telling the truth."

Tom went to meetings of the Herdwick Sheepbreeders with Beatrix, and although he could not attend the meeting, which was private, she usually rejoined him when the business was over. Once, not wishing to attend a dinner connected with a meeting in Cockermouth, she and Tom went instead to a lile cafe just round the corner and each had a cup of tea and a teacake. Tom was to recall that Beatrix, thirsty and impatient, poured some hot tea into a saucer and drank from it like many a working man.

When Mr C T Williamson was a young shepherd in his teens, he was on Eskdale showfield with some Herdwick sheep, making them ready for the show ring. "After two days walking over the tops by Wasdale Head, plus a really wet Lakeland morning, the sheep were not looking at their best. Coming towards me was an odd sight - Mrs Heelis, with a hessian bag around her waist and another folded mid-bottom which covered her head and shoulders; she was definitely waterproofed. Assisted by her shepherd, she was putting the final touches to her Herdwick sheep. These would later be judged by two appointed shepherds along with many more entries.

"I was amazed by the manner in which she went about her job. She was really enjoying it, despite the rain. She knew her beloved Herdwicks and would argue with anyone on their merits. When I hear her name, either mentioned or in print, my thoughts go back to the Eskdale Show incident. She was an odd lady, but was at home with her sheep."

The Last Days

EVEN IN old age, Beatrix - by now dumpy and bent but retaining her cherubic face - had time to spend with the Girl Guides who had been visiting her property from the late 1920s. She had her minor grumbles, such as when the Guides dropped hair "slides", buttons and paper in the hay. The dairymaid deputed to pick over the hay before it reached the mouths of the livestock was allowed to keep the booty.

In the post-war austerity, food was still rationed and Peter Rabbit and his friends had to be especially alert as they were stalked by a hungry populace. A prisoner of war camp for Germans had been established at Grizedale Hall, just over the hill from Sawrey, and in the opposite direction Beatrix's worst fears about pollution from noisy seaplanes were realised when Sunderland Flying Boats, like huge white swans, were flown off the lake from the point just north of Bowness where they were being assembled. One of the lake steamers had been requisitioned as a patrol vessel by the Royal Navy.

The wavering drone of German aircraft, heading for industrial targets like Barrow-in-Furness, made the night air shiver. No naked lights were permitted. There was just the cold light of the moon and the glow from Barrow when bombs had found their destinations. For a few weeks, the Sawrey district blazed with autumnal tints. Then, near Christmas, as Beatrix's life ebbed away, the weather was cold and miserable.

Josephina Banner remembers that towards the end of her life, when "her eyes gave out" and art work was out of the question, even if she had felt inclined to do some, Delmar said to her - "You've never done a book about a lamb, though you've a handy farm and know all about Herdwick sheep." Beatrix had looked wistful, then replied: "Ah, I would have loved to do such a book but my eyes and my hands won't do it." A pause. "I don't think I could have done it. Sheep are the most difficult things of all to draw."

Beatrix visited Heathwaite Farm in Coniston, where Delmar and Josephina were staying. "Her funny old car was too rickety to go up the steep lane, so we met her at the bottom with a milk float and white pony. The step was too high for her so we laid a board across. Delmar held one hand. I held the other little podgy hand. She walked up this board into the float and took the reins and then the milkman's boy held the bridle. There was this wonderful procession up the lonnin [lane] and all the people in the cottages on the way knew about it. She held the reins and went up, quite a long way, and they all waved through the windows. And when we got to Heathwaite Farm, we found that local people had sent bunches of flowers. The farm was full of flowers. Oh - they loved her all right." The Banners provided the lunch. Beatrix had second helpings of everything.

Beatrix and Josephina met for what turned out to be the last time in the garden at Hill Top, Sawrey. They walked beside the flowers, then near the apple trees, then beside the vegetable plot to a strip of ground where wild flowers were to be found. These flowers, which had been collected and planted by Beatrix, included "zig-zag clover", Beatrix's name for a variety of plant she associated with Timmy Willie. He'd waved it to Tommy Town Mouse in one of the famous tales. Now the two ladies walked to the little iron gate set beside mossy posts. Josephina was most moved when Beatrix pulled her head down to her level and kissed her. "Neither of us spoke. We knew, as we parted company, that we would never meet again. When I turned round, there was Beatrix, waving a clover leaf at me. Just as Timmy Willie had done."

A few hours before her death, in December, 1943, Tom Storey was at her bedside. "Mrs Rogerson told me she wanted to see me. Would I come across after I'd finished the farm work? I said: 'Aye, I'll be across'." Tom hand-milked the Shorthorn cows - there were no milking units at Hill Top as long as Beatrix was alive - and he finished about six o'clock. "Then I went into the house and had a wesh and a bite to eat - what we called supper. I didn't change all through, but just put a decent jacket on."

Mrs Rogerson admitted him to Castle Cottage. Willie Heelis was not at home. Beatrix lay in bed "at yon end of t'house." There was no fire in the room. "I sat down and we chatted about farming. She asked how things were going on. I think she thought she was 'going' the way she talked to me that night. One thing she asked me to do - and I thought it was the main thing she had asked me to come across for - was to carry on looking after the farm for Mr Heelis after her day. Years before, I'd had a letter asking me to do the same thing. It had been written in pencil when she was lying in hospital two years before she died."

Tom left Beatrix's bedside at about seven o' clock. "I hadn't stayed long." Beatrix Heelis (nee Potter) died during the night, aged 77. She was cremated on the last day of the year. Tom related how at dinner-time one day early in January, her husband Willie Heelis arrived at Hill Top with her ashes. He brought 'em into the kitchen wrapped in newspaper. He said: "You"ll know where these have to go, Storey." Tom finished his meal, had his usual "sit-down" and then went for a walk with the parcel that Willie Heelis had brought. "It was a bonny day," he recalled. The ashes were reverently scattered on the Hill Top high pastures with, it is theorised, a view of Sawrey and Esthwaite Water.

In its obituary, *The Times* noted that Beatrix Potter had died in the days just before Christmas, "a time at which, for the last forty years, she has been much in the minds of happy children. It is no mean epitaph, and they are legion who think of her gratefully." Delmar Banner, in an appreciation published in the same newspaper on December 30, wrote: "Her many farm tenants all over the dales honoured her as landlord of care and understanding. She was a noted breeder and judge of Herdwick sheep. At all sheep shows could be seen her short, stout, venerable figure, her countenance full of intelligence and humour, her plump, apple-rosy cheeks, and shrewd blue eyes. She was a Cumbrian, solid, realistic, truthful."

To the writer in the *New York Herald Tribune* (issue of January 6, 1944), Beatrix was a "North-Country farmer, connoisseur of old furniture and china, lover of nature and animals...an artist both with words and with brush." Her greatness lay "in the fact that she was able again and again to create that rare thing - a book that brings grown-ups and children together in a shared delight."

In her will, Beatrix bequeathed almost all her possessions to her husband during his lifetime. Sums of money were left to two cousins. Her shares in the publishing firm of Frederick Warne were left to Frederick Warne Stephens. On the death of Willie Heelis, he would also acquire the rights and royalties relating to her books. Remembered in her will were personal friends and helpers, including Tom Storey and her chauffeur Walter Stevens. She instructed that a meadow at Satter Howe, on Ferry Hill, should be kept in memory of local men who perished in the 1914-18 war.

There remained her greatest legacy - 4,300 acres of property, including fourteen farms, to the National Trust. A life interest in the property was invested in William, who quickly and most generously relinquished his interest. Beatrix specified that her rooms at Hill Top, Sawrey, should be kept as she had left them. The house was not to be tenanted. The sheep on her fell farms should continue to be pure Herdwick and there must be no hunting by otter hounds and harriers at Troutbeck Park. Her ultimate gifts to the National Trust were taken for granted and not talked about. She wanted that to be, above all, her legacy to the Lake District.

As for Willie Heelis, at the time Beatrix died he was in a sad physical state, with prostate gland trouble. He refused to go to hospital for an operation and in the end he languished in the Purey Cust nursing home, almost in the shadow of York Minster, where the sonorous notes of the largest bell marked for him the passage of time. Tom Storey went to see him just before he died in 1945. On his return, he told his family: "I could tell he was a long way on..."

The memory of Beatrix Potter has not faded in the half century and more since her death. Anyone who is steeped in the lore of this astonishing woman, when visiting Near Sawrey, half expects to see her stocky little figure hurrying along Stony Lane or, at Troutbeck Park, sitting on The Tongue, alert to the sights and sounds of the fells. Anyone who reads her books discovers there is magic in ordinary things - in rabbits and ducks, rhubarb patches and water-butts, white-washed cottages and lily-covered tarns, roadside flowers, pigs and goats and, of course, in Herdwick sheep.

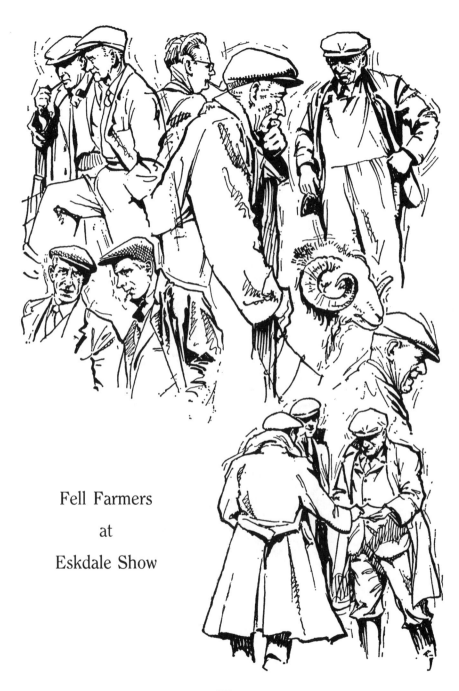

Fell Farmers
at
Eskdale Show

111

The Tales of Beatrix Potter

1901   *The Tale of Peter Rabbit.*

Inspired by a picture-letter sent to Noel Moore. The old garden at Fawe Park, near Keswick, where Beatrix stays with her family, provides some details of Mr McGregor's garden. This, the first of her little books, is printed privately in December, with a run of 250 copies. (A second edition of 200 copies will follow in February, 1902 and in October 1902 the book will appear under the Warne imprint, with colour illustrations. The first printing of 8,000 copies is sold before publication at a retail cost of 1s. A Peter Rabbit doll which she makes is registered at the Patent Office in 1903).

1903   *The Tailor of Gloucester.*

Based on John Samuel Prichard, who was indeed a tailor at Gloucester. The book is printed privately, with a run of 500 copies. (and subsequently shortened for the edition published by Warne).

1903   *The Tale of Squirrel Nutkin.*

Had its first telling in one of Beatrix's picture-letters, this being posted to Norah Moore in 1901. At the time of writing, Beatrix is holidaymaking at Lingholm. She has borrowed back the letter and uses it as the basis of her book. She has been less familiar with a red squirrel than with a rabbit. When the gamekeeper fails to get her a squirrel, she sketches from an animal bought in a pet shop. The notion of squirrels crossing water on rafts of bark, using their bushy tails as sails, appears to have been inspired by reading a book about Canadian wildlife. The setting chosen by Beatrix is Derwentwater, with views of "the Queen of

English Lakes". St Herbert's Island is the inspiration for Owl Island, presided over by the owl himself, Mr Brown. The oak tree from which he keeps a watching brief on the nut crop is sketched from life in Fawe Park, just north of Lingholm, where the Potters have stayed for family holidays.

1904   *The Tale of Benjamin Bunny.*
        The dedication is "for the children of Sawrey from Old Mr Bunny." In the pictures are features painted by Beatrix in 1903 when the Potter family was staying at Lingholm and Fawe Park, overlooking Derwentwater.

1904   *The Tale of Two Bad Mice.*
        In which Tom Thumb and Hunca Munca raid a doll's house, the house itself being based on one made for Winifred Warne, and dedicated to her as W M L W, "the little girl who had the doll's house." The book is published in time for the Christmas market. Warnes confidently print 30,000 copies.

1905   *The Tale of Mrs Tiggy-Winkle.*
        The setting for this story of a hedgehog-washerwoman is

Catbells, near Keswick. In the story is a reference to Skelghyl, alias Skelgill Farm, the home of Lucie Carr. The book is dedicated to "the real little Lucie of Newlands,", this being one of the daughters of the Vicar of Newlands. Beatrix's drawing is of Littletown, in Newlands, a little to the south. The model for Mrs Tiggy-Winkle was a pet hedgehog she took with her on her travels housed in a cardboard box.

1905   *The Pie and the Patty-pan.*
Published initially in larger size format, with a frontispece including a view of Hill Top, Sawrey.

1906   *The Tale of Mr Jeremy Fisher.*
The germ of the idea is yet another picture-letter, this time a missive sent to Eric Moore, when the Potters were staying at Dunkeld, beside the silvery Tay. Beatrix had kept frogs as pets. She knew all about their anatomy, both inside and out, having dissected some. The setting of the tale is switched to Esthwaite Water, between Sawrey and Hawkshead.

1906   *The Story of a Fierce Bad Rabbit.*
Panoramic form - i.e., a production with the pages connected horizontally and opening like a concertina.

1906   *The Story of Miss Moppet.*
Panoramic Form.

1907   *The Tale of Tom Kitten.*
The cat on which she modelled Tom is borrowed from friends living at Windermere. The setting is Hill Top, Sawrey, and its garden, both of which are smothered in flowers. Mrs Tabitha Twitchit led Tom, Mittens and Moppet up the long, flagged path to Hill top and, inside the house, she washed and dressed them. Beatrix took great pride in the interiors, with their oaken furnishings, picked up at various sales and arranged by her to maxium effect.

1908   *The Tale of Jemima Puddle-Duck.*
This is, in effect, a re-telling of the sad tale of Little Red Riding Hood. Beatrix, who is fond of fairy tales, dedicates this update to Ralph and Betsy Cannon, of Hill Top, using the house and its locality as the setting and including a picture featuring her dog Kep. Also pictured is the Tower Bank Arms, with its prominent, clock-adorned porch.

1908   *The Roly-Poly Pudding.*
Dedicated to a pet rat which Beatrix owned in childhood. On purchasing Hill Top, she finds it over-run with rats. Mrs Cannon is reported to have seen a rat "sitting up eating its dinner under the kitchen table." First published in larger size format, then in the familiar small size, this work is subsequently re-named *The Tale of Samuel Whiskers.* It features the real life Farmer Postlethwaite, of Near Sawrey. Beatrix's painting of him in a rat-ravaged barn is based on a photograph she had taken. It was only partly successful. Postlethwaite turned his back on the camera.

1909   *Ginger and Pickles.*
Later changed to *The Tale of Ginger and Pickles.* The central

feature is the shop at Near Sawrey. In Beatrix's narrative appear some of the old familiar characters, including Samuel Whiskers, Jeremy Fisher and Jemima Puddle-duck. First published in larger size format.

1910 *The Tale of Mrs Tittlemouse.*
Not a house mouse, but a wood mouse, and one which is described by Beatrix as being tidy and particular. The story is written for Nellie, the youngest daughter of Harold Warne.

1911 *Peter Rabbit's Painting Book.*

1911 *The Tale of Timmy Tiptoes.*
A story featuring a grey squirrel, introduced into the English countryside from America. With American readers in mind, Beatrix draws a black bear and two chipmunks - Mr and Mrs Chippy Hackee.

1912 *The Tale of Mr Tod.*
He is a fox, a denizen of the Sawrey area.

1913 *The Tale of Pigling Bland.*
Beatrix introduces the female pig into literature. For her illustrations, she spent some time with a pig inside its sty. The county bridge (Lancashire/Westmorland) at Colwith, near Elterwater, is crossed at speed by Pigling Bland and Pig-wig.

1918 *The Tale of Johnny Town-Mouse.*
Her first book for five years. The "town" is Hawkshead.

1929   *The Fairy Caravan.*

Printed privately, with a run of 100 copies. Inspired by seeing Ginnet's Travelling Circus at Ambleside. Codlin Croft is modelled on Low Lindeth Farm. The impulse to write this book came during one of her visits to Troutbeck Tongue. Some of the illustrations are based on Beatrix's own farm at Troutbeck Park. Charcoal-burners in the woodland of Graythwaite, west of Windermere, are believed to have inspired the creation of the diminutive Oakmen.

A Bibliography

Cumbria magazine (New Series, beginning in 1951)

Davies, Hunter, *A Walk Round the Lakes* (1979); *Beatrix Potter's Lakeland* (1988)

Heelis, John, *The Tale of Mrs William Heelis - Beatrix Potter* (1993)

Lane, Margaret, *The Magic Years of Beatrix Potter* (1978)

Linder, Leslie, *The Journal of Beatrix Potter* (1966, since revised)

Mitchell, W R, *Beatrix Potter Remembered* (1987)

Parker, Ulla Hyde, *Cousin Beatie* (1981)

Rice, H A L, *Lake Country Echoes* (1973)

Taylor, Judy, *Beatrix Potter, Artist, Storyteller and Countrywoman* (1986); *That Naughty Rabbit* (1987); *Beatrix Potter's Letters* (1989).